MY MOTHER TOLD ME

By

Madge Millard-Brawn.

Copyright 2008 Madge Brawn

ISBN: 978-0-9559740-0-7

MY MOTHER TOLD ME

INTRODUCTION

There is in the kitchen cupboard above the fridge a lampshade; it is just an ordinary lampshade, frosted orange glass with flowers around the bell shape. To me it is very special; my mother bought it the year I was born from my Uncle Ivan who was, at that time, a lamp-oil man. That makes it 74years old, not quite an antique but it is in better shape than I am at this moment, at least it isn't cracked and it sparkles when washed.

Some of this is about me when I was small, Mother told me most of the memories, but I do remember some of the things myself. Things vaguely come from the back of my mind and I seem to remember though my sister will say I remembered it all wrong. But as they are from my memory you must make up your own mind and enjoy them just the same They are also from memories I have through the years, so it's from what My Mother told Me to What I am Remembering right or wrong.

Mother told my husband a lot of things, as she delighted in talking about 'Our Madge'. Her favourite saying was 'There is nothing normal about Our Madge, she always surprises you when you least expect it'.

So, here goes, enjoy tales my mother told me, and my own memories.

Chapter 1. EARLY DAYS.

When Mother and Father were first married he was a bread rounds man with a van pulled by a horse and cart, the horse knew the way round and when and where to stop. Dad was able to leave the horse to do its own thing and jump on and off the van when necessary. I don't know what the horse was called but he knew who would give him a crust or where to find a drink of water. The pay wasn't much so Dad changed his job and became an Insurance Man. Till then the horse supplied us with the essential additive to the allotment which supplied us with fresh veg. and eggs, for my Dad kept hens as well.

We lived in a two up two down terraced house with a yard at the back. At the top of the yard was the outside toilet or Privy as it was know in those days and still is on some occasions. My Grandmother would say "Am jest gwin t't petty' meaning 'I'm just going to the toilet' you needed two languages in our family as my Grandparents were 'reet Lankie' (right Lancashire). Going to the Loo (how many names are there for the toilet?) in the middle of winter was a major expedition, you either had to run like ---- and sit there shivering or get dressed as if going to the North Pole, but it was something we were used to and thought nothing of it. Many's the time we have stood with our backs to the fire after a trip up the yard.

We had a front room, the parlour, kept for best when we had visitors, a kitchen where Mother did all the baking, washing, ironing etc and where we had our meals. Before Mother was married she couldn't boil water and had to ask the lady next door how to do the washing. She told me it took her ages to light the fire to heat the water in the back boiler. 'I used to think I would never finish, washing on Monday, ironing on Tuesday, baking on Wednesday, (I forget what she said she did on Thursday probably shopping), cleaning on Friday and looking after you two in between times Weekly shop was done on Saturday's with a visit to the market, the Sunday was church, where my Dad played the organ and we had to get dressed in our Sunday Best.

In spite of all the work she found time to go to night school and learn to be a Milliner, stopping just before she took her City and Guilds Certificate, she told me she was afraid of not passing. She was too good for that to happen.

Friday night was bath nigh. Down would come the zinc bath which hung behind the kitchen door, it was filled with buckets full of hot water and we would sit one at each end in front of the kitchen fire and be washed all over with glycerine soap. My hair being fair was rinsed with camomile tea; Brenda's was rinsed with vinegar to make it shine as hers was a shade darker than mine. My Godparents Auntie Florrie and Uncle Frank came nearly every Friday night to give us a bath. There was water every where. Splashing and bubbles were the order of the day. It all had to be finished by 6.30pm as that was bed time, although we were allowed up a little later on this special day as hair had to be washed and put in curl rags. Our hair was naturally curly but mother had to have everything in order and ringlets were the order of the day

Uncle Ivan was, as I said a 'lamp-oil man' when he was young and first married to my Aunt Clara, Dad's older sister. In case you don't know what a lamp-oil man was, he was someone with a horse and cart who sold paraffin oil along with donkey stone both yellow and white which the house wives used to clean their steps, dolly blue wrapped in bandage type material with a little wooden stick in the middle which was used to blue the last rinsing water of the weekly wash to make it sparkling white He also sold dusters. light bulbs, gas mantles & candles in case there was a power cut. In other words items you can't get now and other things you can get from the hardware or ironmongers. (Do they still have ironmongers?) Every Monday he would come along our street shouting 'lampull' (lamp oil) and the ladies would go out with their cans for their oil lamps along with baskets to put the rest of their good in. If you saw it today it would look like a museum piece. Some of the things have already been on the Antiques Show, am I really so old? What is a Donkey Stone? Try to describe that to an eight year old. 'Why scrub your steps, Grandma? Didn't you just sweep them?'

The housewives were very proud of their front of house. Every morning they would sweep the pavement and clean or mop the steps with yellow donkey stone finishing off with a white edge to the step. Then the brass would be polished, if there was any, rubbed until you could see your face in it. This done they could go to the shops with their heads held high and look down their nose at those who had a dirty front, they let down the standard of the street. People were very proud in those days and took great care of things. Money may have been scarce but there was plenty of pride, 'Soap and water is cheap enough' they used to say, 'and elbow grease cost nothing'.

It was quite common to see people sat on the steps in the evening, if the weather was nice. In those days it was a meeting place where all the gossip could be passed along from house to house growing with every telling of it." Did you see Mrs. ---- with her new fur tippet? And her hasn't got two ha'pnies to rub t'gether. A wunder how who paid fer that?" " M-m-m-, tut- tut".

The stairs in our house went up in between the two rooms to a little landing with a door either side. The front bedroom was were mum and dad slept and the back was ours. Brenda & I had a big double bed with a flock mattress and loads and loads of blankets topped off with an eiderdown.

Making the bed involved a lot of hard work and once a week the mattress was taken outside and shaken till it was fluffy again. My Mother told me the blankets were hung out of the windows to keep them smelling sweet and fresh.

My sister Brenda was 3 ½ years older than me and I slept with her in the double bed until the day I married, so have rarely slept on my own except on the few occasions when my husband went away on business or I went to college, but that is far in the future and a good few years have to be gone through before we reach that time in my life..

Our house was within the sound of the football ground where my father went every Saturday when they played at home. He went with his friend Jo Cooper. Jo, his wife Hilda, their children Frank and Hilda lived in the house just across the street and they were friends with Mother & Father until the time my Father died. We went to all sorts of places together, day trips to the park being the main one. We would take a picnic with sandwiches and lemonade, when we could afford it as a special treat, otherwise water was in the bottles Dad carried. My Mother told me we had loads of fun all four of us playing together, Frank being the eldest and me the youngest, I was always 'it' when' it' came to hide and seek. I never could find anyone and have hated it ever since.

Father played the piano in the pub to make some extra money. I never learned to read music but could pick out a tune by ear, I loved to stand by him when he played and stand on a stool so that I could turn the pages when he told me. Most of all I loved to sing and dance to the music, even though I didn't know the words. I never learned how to read music properly but could follow the tune just by the way the notes were written on the paper. Dad said I had an ear for music, whatever that meant.

Mother wasn't too keen on Dad playing the piano, and would say 'Do you have to, Harold?' whenever he sat down to play. I think this is why he went to play in the pub, this way he could play and no one said 'do you have to' Mother hated the violin especially, she said it screeched, music wasn't her forte, though she grew to like it, musicals more than anything. Surprising how our tasted change over the years. When I was older Mother my sister & I used to go to the pictures where we sat through many a Fred Astair and Ginger Rogers movie.

Grandfather and Grandmother lived in a house similar to ours in a town nearby. There was initially my father. Harold, and his two sisters, one older than him called Clara (who married the lamp-oil man) and one younger called Agnes. Grandmother & Grandfather had previously had a grocers shop and even went to Switzerland to see how chocolate was made. Quite an adventure in the years between the wars, the journey was by rail and sea I don't know how long it took them but it was quite a trip or so my Mother told me.

Their house was in a terrace as were most of the houses in those days. The back was a communal space with a separate toilet for each house. There was a washing line which ran down the whole length of the yard which everyone shared Grandma & Granddad had a swing attached to the lintel of their toilet which I loved until the day I fell out of it and got concussion from the concrete flags underneath. "Hers cracked 'er 'eead" I can remember Grandma saying. "Nowts broken, but who'll 'ave a mighty 'eeadache." This translates as "She has cracked her head. Nothing is broken but she will have a mighty headache" They were 'reet Lankie' (right Lancashire)

Mother told me that when I was very young she & Dad used to wrap bandages dipped in melted Vaseline around my legs and feet, to stop them from cracking as I had such delicate skin. At times it flaked off like fish scales.

I found out much later when working for a doctor as his secretary, that the top layer of my skin was missing making it very dry and subject to cracking especially round my heels and finger tips, and behind my ears, all the tender places which were very sore especially in the winter or drying winds.

I was given all sorts of medicines to see if it could be cured, even some which were given to horses to make their coat shine, these had to be crushed and given to me one-eighth per day. Also I had a very bad bronchitis and Mother would make a liberty bodice covered in Thermogene wool which I had to wear all winter and when spring finally arrived she would peel the wool off layer by layer so that I wouldn't catch cold. Thermogene wool was like cotton wool in sheet form soaked with some kind of medicament like mentholatum or wintergreen which stunk. "Tha' stinks summat awful" everyone could tell I was coming from the smell of it. It gradually wore off thank goodness, you got used to it in time.

I remember one birthday, I must have been three years old, when I got up the whole street was decorated with streamers and bunting together with many other kinds of decoration. The skies were blue and I skipped up and down the pavement singing, imagine my disappointment when someone told me they weren't for me but for Empire Day, which was later in the month and they were just practicing to get it right for the big day.

Nevertheless when the day came we had a good time with a huge street party with lots to eat including jelly and custard. The street was lined with tables, everyone bringing their big kitchen table out with the best linen, all snowy white; it had been scrubbed specially for the day. We ate and sang songs and danced till night time .Brenda and I were allowed up late that night. It made my birthday very special; we don't have Empire Day any more, mores the pity.

There was a real feeling of a big family where everyone cared for everyone else. You could leave the front door unlocked and be sure no one would go in unless asked.

My big sister had a tricycle with a sidecar attached. I don't know whether Mum & Dad bought it or had it made especially for us, but I never saw another one like it nor have I done since. We used to ride all over the place on the trike, up and down the street visiting the neighbours. At the top of the street in the very end house lived our Aunt Mary and Uncle Albert, they had a son, John who was a little older than my big sister he was so tall I felt I was looking up at a giant. My Aunt and Uncle were both tall, Uncle was Grandmother's brother and all her side of the family were like giants, not only tall but big with it. Father wasn't tall at all, he was only 5ft.10in so I guess the gene must have slipped by him because I am only little. At times it was like living in Brobdingnag. Two doors down from us lived a couple who I loved to visit regularly, even after we moved, she was what you would call these days a craftswoman. Every time you went into the house she was making something, she showed me how to make paper beads on a winding tool, paint flowers on black velvet turning them into cushions when they were dry. We dipped candles and made soft toys, all manner of things some useful some just for fun. 'Time is too precious to waste on making mischief' she used to tell me, 'spend your time wisely making yourself happy and you will make others happy too' I suppose she had a bigger influence on me than I thought as even now I hate to sit idle and do nothing.

Surprising how things remind you of something else at the oddest time. I was painting a picture of some poppies and I suddenly remembered Mrs.????? But, couldn't remember her name., all I could think was that she was such a nice lady.

Father had an allotment where he grew all manner of vegetables and flowers, he also kept hens which Mother couldn't' stand, she was terrified of them. She hated the clucking noise they made and was frightened to death when one came scratching round her feet. When she had to feed them for one reason or another she would send my sister and I in to do it. She would flap her pinny at them to keep them away and if one of them bubbled as they do when they are broody she would run out of the pen with her pinny over her head. Poor mother had so many phobias we teased her about them all the time.

Father was very proud of his flowers, carnations were his favourites, and he grew them in rows all down the path in the allotment. One day when my sister and I had cycled down to the 'plot' she decided to pick all the heads off the flowers and stick them in the ground next to each plant.

Boy! was she in trouble when Dad found out, he took the strap to her, three whacks on her bare bottom, that was his standard punishment, Dad with a very severe face and Mum with her pinny over her head crying,' No, Harold, don't, no, no,' Then she would fold us up in her arms, wipe the tears away with her still wet pinny and say, 'There, there,' to make it better.

The only thing in my sister's defence was that she wanted there to be more flowers for Dad to be proud of. When I tell this tale,

Brenda always says "You can't remember that, you weren't born yet" Though as she is only 3 ½ years older than me she must have been very young to have done it on her own. Some of it is from memory and some as my Mother told me.

Mother's mother, my maternal Grandmother, died when Mother was eight and her Father, my Grandfather disappeared the after the funeral, leaving Mother in the care of her Grandfather & Grandmother Bolton. She led a very sheltered life and wasn't allowed a bike. "Tha'll cum whom killt" translation "You will come home killed" nor was she allowed to learn how to swim,"Tha'll cum whom drowndéd" I don't think that needs a translation. But in spite of not being allowed to do so many things, she finished up a super mum with a great sense of humour, but you could tease her and she would believe anything you told her. She lived with her 6 Aunts as well as Grandma & Grandpa Bolton, the tales she told me about her Grandma still make me laugh.

Grandma Bolton was only tiny or so Mother told me, she wore a shawl and clogs all the time. One time when she decided to whitewash the kitchen ceiling, she stood on the kitchen table, brush in hand and walked straight of the end of the table, falling bottom first into the dolly tub. "It rolled me down't yard and tipped mi out int't suff" meaning she rolled down the back yard until the tub tipped her out into the grid at the bottom.

Then there was the time when they went to the pictures and sat at the front on wooden benches sucking Uncle Joes Mint Balls, her with her clogs and shawl and Grandfather Bolton with his billycock hat on. Aunt Ethel and Uncle John, Mothers Aunt and Uncle would sit at the back on chairs pretending they didn't belong as Aunt Ethel thought she was better the others when she married Uncle John, "Who'se getten above hersen," Grandma Bolton would say according to what Mother told me, meaning 'She is getting above herself, she thinks she is better than us.' Then at the end of the picture show, Grandmother Bolton would take off her clogs and tying the laces together, fling them over her shoulders and gaily walk all the way home in her stocking feet.

Whenever a friend of Mothers called Nellie Glennie had something new, Mother had to have it too, only better. " If Nelly's getten a watch, tha munt hev one too, only non o' thet sil'er stuff, that munt hev gowd" So saying she would march to the jewellers where she would only deal with the manager or owner and buy Mother the best gold watch she could afford. If Nellie had a fur tippet Mother would have to have a fur tippet, but in spite of this Mother and Nellie were the best of friends. Mother never did find out why or how her Grandmother knew the managers of nearly all the shops, but she would only deal with them.

Nellie's Mother was a 'case'. According to mother if she was washing and things just didn't go according to plan she would say "They don't went t'bi weshed t'day, A'll leave it till thi do." And so saying she would up and away and leave everything until she felt more inclined to do it. The same with any housework, but it got done in the end.

Mother learned to be an excellent seamstress and made all our clothes. When we went on holiday, which we did every year in spite of the tight budget, Mother used to spend the weeks beforehand making our dresses. A dress for each day we were away - that meant if we went away for one week 14 dresses and 14 pairs of knickers to match. She even made our coats and hats with material which she got from the local market, all this on a treadle machine with none of the modern gadgets that make it easy these days .The buttonholes had to be stitched by hand, the trimming was painstakingly undertaken, rouleaux and ruches, frills and flounces, no stitch missed until it was finished. She took great pride in her work and loved to see us 'turned out looking pretty, just like the little princesses'. Not bad for someone who when she was first married couldn't boil water and had to ask one of the neighbours to show her how to do the washing

One of Mothers favourite tales about me was the first time they took us to the seaside. Dad was loaded up as usual with deck chairs and mother had the food, costumes, towels and all the other things people took to the beach. Whilst they were setting up things for the day Mother let go my hand in the hope that I would play in the sand, "Be a good little girl like your big sister" she told me, BUT NO. When they found time to look round to see how we were going on I had marched down the beach towards the sea, another minute and I would have been up to my neck in water. Mother couldn't run fast enough to stop me, and believe me Mother never ran anywhere if she could help it. She often said 'there is nothing normal about our Madge.' I was called Madge because mother did not like nick-names and rather than call me Margaret or Marjorie only have it shortened to Madge was something she didn't want, so Madge it was. Short for nothing but me.

Dad on the other hand would try his hand at anything. Show him a box of tools and he was in his element, I think I must take after him because I am the one they buy tools for on birthdays and Christmas. He did all the painting as his friend Jo Cooper was a painter and decorator, he taught Dad the tricks of the trade. In turn Dad taught me, it was fun getting the papers straight and putting a good finish on the paint.

Father and Mother before their aged 3yrs

Brenda aged 6 yrs, me

Chapter 2. THE SHOP

When I was 4 yrs old we moved from the 2 up 2 down into a sweets and tobacconists shop and Dad bought a car. The car, an Austin 7, was called Jenny and we went everywhere in her weekends and holidays. Dad told me he never had a driving lesson, as it wasn't obligatory in those days. His Mother had bought a Lagonda car and just given him the keys and told him to drive it. That was how they learned to drive "Practice will mak' thee perfect", Grandma told him.. Mother never wanted to learn and would scream if ever she were asked to get behind the wheel when Dad needed some assistance. She would do her usual and cover her face with her hands, it may go away if she couldn't see it, whatever it was.

Our first holiday away in the car was to Rhyl in North Wales, previously we had been to Fleetwood or Cleveleys, and places we could get to easily by train. Going on our holidays by car was a great adventure, it took forever and the journey was always interesting, non of the "Are we there yet?" Mother liked to look at the houses as we went past and would imagine what it would be like to live in some of them especially the ones with a bathroom and big kitchen.

We were loaded up with luggage, mother packed everything but the kitchen sink, just in case. 'You never know what the weather will do, and we don't want to be caught short.' We eventually got to the boarding house, it was one where we rented the room and the landlady would cook the food we provided, mainly for breakfast and evening meal. The rest of the time we had sandwiches made by mother. Going down to the beach was a day out on its own, we had to carry deck chairs, picnic equipment, towels, bathing suits, hair brushes, hats in case it was sunny

There were of course lots of other things which Mother thought essential for a day on the sands. Of course my sister and I had to carry our share of things not forgetting the essential bucket and spade. Rhyll at that time was a quiet place but it did have entertainment for the holidaymakers. There was, every week, a competition for the Holiday Queen and one for Young Miss Rhyll. Mother wanted to enter both Brenda and me, but my big sister came over all shy as usual so it was left to me to go onto stage which I didn't mind one bit. Surprise, surprise, I won, there was a picture of me in the local paper which mother kept in her scrapbook, she still had it when she died. We went to Rhyl for three years running and each year mother entered me in the Miss Rhyl contest, luckily I was the winner each time.. Makes me sound big headed, but I enjoyed it. It was fun, There wasn't a big prize, a few shillings or a toy, I can't remember, nothing much, just the fun of entering. Except for the last time.

When we went to the beach in the morning before the contest and as usual we played in the sand, I wandered off down to the sea and

Mum & Dad thought I was waving to them kneeling down in the surf but I wasn't, I was shouting for help as I was sinking lower and lower in quicksand.

A young couple was walking past and pulled me out. I shudder to think what would have happened if they hadn't been there, as by then I was up to my waist in quicksand, I went back to Mother & Father in tears. They were so shocked to think that they had just sat there thinking I was having fun in the rock pools, it doesn't bear thinking about. It still has an effect on me even now, I hate anything tight and being in small spaces i.e. a lift is something that still makes me shudder.

Mother took me back to the boarding house to clean me up. "Oh, our Madge. Whatever will you do next? You'll be the death of me if you don't take more care" Poor Mother didn't quite know what to do to make it right. The worst thing for me was that I had to wear the dress I had on the day before as the special one mother had made for the competition had been ruined in the quicksand.

I still came first in the Little Miss Rhyll Contest but we never went back to Rhyl after that. The picture they took afterwards wasn't as happy a picture as the ones that had been taken after the other contests, can you wonder?

The shop was on the main road across from the Railway goods yard and even though it was so close I don't recall hearing the shunting very often, it must have been because of the big wall that surrounded it. It was also across the side street from the primary school where my sister and I first went to school, I suppose she must have gone to school before me, as she is 3 ½ yrs older than I am but I don't remember that bit.

Whilst waiting to go to school one day, we were stood on the step of the shop when my teacher Miss Pearce, walked past, looking at me and Mother she said 'Someone has sent me a Meg', Mother laughed, ' I wonder who you mean?' she replied. I hadn't a clue what they were talking about.

The teacher must have been in her early twenties but to me she seemed quite old. I remember her primping her hair between her fingers; I guess it must have been the early form of backcombing. Miss Pearce and Miss Jones those are the two teachers who stand out most in my memory. We had Miss Jones for music where I was a dab hand on the triangle.

Primary school was a happy time. My one fear was of being sent to see the head master, you would have to stand outside his door till your name was called and if you had been very naughty your name would go in The Big Black Book. What happened after that I never did find out, as I never got sent to see the Headmaster, just the thought of it was enough.

We sold all sorts of sweets and chocolate some you can even buy today like flying saucers, except they weren't called that in those days. My favourites were fondant horse shoes made into a kind of box, in each one was a little gift, a ring or dice or some such trinket. There was one box in every carton with a silver three penny bit inside; I used to shake all the horseshoes to see if I could fine THE one. Sometimes I did and sometimes I didn't. One Christmas

I asked for a box of Cadbury penny chocolate bars, I liked to suck them till they went pointed. Yum, yum.

It was when I was about 8yrs old that a gentleman came in the shop and I went in to the shop to 'help' as I did when mother was busy. The man at the other side of the counter asked to see my mother, I asked for his name as I had been taught to do in case it was someone she didn't want to see. We all do it don't we? The man said "Tell her it's her Father", which surprised me, as I never thought of her as having a father, he had never been mentioned. I went in the back and told her that her father was here to see her and she went in the shop. That is the one and only time I had seen my grandfather. I never did find out what they talked about. It wasn't till mother was in her 70's that she found out he had married again and she had step-relations she never knew about and never did. All her life, or most of it Mother thought she was the only one, her family was very dear to her and she needed us all to be with her on special occasions. Thinking about it later, this explained a lot about Mother, things that you take for granted as a child.

As I mentioned earlier my Father played the piano and I loved to dance when he played, so mother decided to send me to dancing class where I took tap and ballet, I loved them both, but mainly ballet. Mother took me to Eileen MacDonald's School of Dance, over the Co-op at Rhodes Bank. I was lucky enough to be able to pick up routines after one or two classes, I loved it, dancing took over from then on.

It didn't take me long to get to be quite good. (Just like me, sounding big headed again.) As a matter of fact if the war hadn't come along I was going to enter for the Royal Ballet School, I wouldn't have been able to go anyway because I was too short. Pity. The story of my life – too short, not my life, just me.

The war came just I had gone on holiday with my Aunt Agnes & Uncle Willie. My Great Aunt & Uncle really as she was the youngest in the family of six girls who were my mother Aunts, the ones she was brought up with. They, my Great Aunt & Uncle, usually took me away for a few days each year having no children of their own. We had only been in Blackpool two or three days when 'WAR BROKE OUT'. My Uncle phoned my father and my father came to pick us up to take us home in the car. It upset me greatly as I couldn't understand why we had to go home straight away without finishing our holiday. War is rotten when it breaks up your holiday. I was 9yrs. old at the time. Being in a sweet shop at the start of the war was no fun especially when sweets became rationed and we had to count out the coupons to send away each week, they were so tiny they blew away in a puff of wind and got all over the place.

We had to cut them out of the ration books as they weren't perforated or anything sophisticated like that. We sold tobacco and cigarettes as well. I remember the smell of the thick twist as it was cut with the guillotine. It smelled nicer than it tasted. You could buy a single cigarette or a pack of 5, 10 or 20 if you had enough money. They didn't seem to be rationed as much as sweets were, or maybe because I didn't smoke the impact wasn't as great.

My other Aunt & Uncle, father's younger sister, (another Aunt Agnes) & Uncle Sid were not exactly bombed out of their home but had to leave it for quite a while whilst it was being made safe. They came to stay with us, why us I do not know, we only had two bedrooms. All I know was though Aunt Clara had more room they wouldn't stay there. Brenda and I together with my two cousins Beryl & Colin slept on mattresses under the stairs, so that Aunt & Uncle could have our bed. It was fun and a games for a while, but you soon gat fed up of squashing together with no room to turn over.

My Dad was an Air raid warden, which meant he got to wear a tin hat. We helped to make the Identity Cards for everyone in the district and I still remember my Number even after all these years. He had to make sure everyone was in the air raid shelter at the bottom of the street. Sitting in one of those all night was agony so we soon got fed up with that. As you can gather from my remembrances about the war, we didn't live anywhere near to the bad bits. The closest we were was the goods yard across the road, but apart from that we had it pretty easy.

That is until my big cousin John got killed in Italy. It was so sad. I remember him coming to the shop and picking up Mother and swinging her round till she collapsed in laughter. We missed him sorely and I think about him even now, not only on Remembrance Day. He died saving his officer's life in Monte Casino.

His Father, Uncle Albert was also an Air Raid Warden and told us about one night when he was on watch and saw parachutes coming down. He said that he watched this one come down in between the two rows of houses at the back. It got caught on the telegraph poles and he saw something swing. Thinking it was a

German soldier he took a big stick and was just about to clout him when he realised that it was a land mine. " A were just about ter lamp 'im one, then a saw wot it were .A ran like billy-oh, A can tell thi" Uncle Albert told us that there were a lot of land mines and unexploded bombs all round the football ground and Hospital, some were near Aunt Clara's too. It was after this that we had Aunt Agnes and her family to stay with us.

Our shop was next door but one to the Doctors. We had two Doctors, Dr. Haliday & Dr, Orr both Scottish, they ran a penny scheme whereby you paid a small amount each week and this paid for any treatment you needed. It was very handy in those days. We got very friendly with both Doctors and I went frequently to their nursery to have tea with the children. The Nanny would make us drop scones or scotch pancakes, which we ate with golden syrup, not good for your teeth but Oh! So nice. Their house was a large Victorian house, the sort the overlookers in the cotton mills used to live in. There was plenty of room for the Surgery and waiting room for the patients at the front with kitchens and dispensary at the back. Up stairs were their living rooms and the nursery.

A few houses up the road was a green grocer where we had all sorts of unusual things, nowadays they are everyday things but then they were quite new. We had Chinese gooseberries even before they became Kiwi fruit, and prawns, and crayfish tails. I remember one day we had samples of baked beans in little paper dishes, they were so good we kept going back for "more please" My sister will say that he was too mean to give us anything, but I remember the baked beans and can still taste them, they haven't changed a bit.

We travelled in the car when Dad could get petrol, the bus and train otherwise. Usually we managed a holiday away once a year even if it meant saving up the petrol coupons. After the episode at Rhyl we went all the way to Bude just at the start of the war, before the holiday when my Aunt Agnes & Uncle Willie had us brought home when war broke out. I went surfing, can you believe it all those years ago, surfing, of course the boards were nothing like they are now, just made of plywood curved at the end. You couldn't stand up on them, just lie down and catch the waves; they call it body surfing now. Great fun. I think that was the farthest we went on holiday until after the war. The picture is of Brenda & me posing at Bude

Usually we went to Blackpool or Fleetwood, which were within an easy journey and didn't take too much petrol. Cleveleys wasn't too far away so we went there too.

I still went to dancing school and loved every minute, my life was one long dance; I danced everywhere, upstairs and downstairs, and in the street just about anywhere where my feet touched the ground. I loved it. It was about this time that my, Mother made my tutu, my very first ballet dress, and I helped. Yards and yards of white net, sticking out from my waist like an upturned mushroom," A reet good twizzer" Grandma said. This was my first attempt at sewing on the machine, it was a treadle machine and I could just reach the treadle to make it go. Mother made it rattle and sewed very fast I tried hard to do the same but usually finished up with a needle and thread doing the hemming and sewing on zips or buttons.

We used to have end of term concerts when we had to work very hard at our routines, both tap and ballet. This was the time when I could dance my heart out, doing solo's, wonderful. I remember one tap routine which I did with five other girls, it was supposed to be in a milk bar and the song was something about milk shakes. There was a bit of dialogue, the only bit I can remember was "I would like a roll". Answer, "Well get on the floor and I'll push you", this got a laugh from the mums and dads, I never knew why.

When I was 11 yrs old it was time for me to take my Grammar School Exam. I knew if I passed I would have to go to the same school as my big sister, I didn't want to go to the same school as her, as I knew everything I did would be compared with her. She didn't want me to go there either. "I'm not going if Our Madge is going" was her usual cry. I thought, if she did needlework, I had to do needlework whether I liked it or not, if she did German, I had to do German and so on and so on. I rebelled and failed the entrance exam deliberately. My teachers and the examination board were so amazed that I had failed the exam that they gave me an Intelligence test. Trust me to come up with one of the highest I.Q. results they had seen, so in the end I still went to the same high school as my big sister. Ah well! You can't have it all your own way. My Mother told me," Just get on with it and hope it turns out better than you thought it would".

This particular day, I was twelve, I was sat on the lid of my desk in break when someone pushed me from behind, just in fun, and I slid off the desk catching my shin on the upturned seat. Looking down I saw a hole in my black woollen stockings, (I had to wear them because of my 'delicate' skin,) through the hole I could see my shinbone; the seat had pushed the flesh up leaving a gap. Surprisingly there was very little blood and no pain, but what a mess, there was quite a big hole once I had taken down my stocking with a roll of flesh pushed up by the seat. Teacher had to send for my Father to take me home where Dr.Orr stitched me up, ten stitches and they had to hold me down whilst they did it.

I hated needles then and still do, they fill me with dread. No going to casualty in those days, the G.P. did things like that in the surgery or in my case at home. I was supposed not to dance for two weeks, or so they thought, I was caught tap dancing just to see if I could still do it and I could, thank goodness the stitches held or I would have had to go through it all again. I still have the scar on my shin to this day and it hurts like H--- if I knock it.

All went well after that going to school, dancing, doing my homework, dancing, helping in the shop, dancing, I lived for dancing; everywhere I went it was done in time to music sung in my head, that is until my dance teacher was called up into the forces and disappeared out of my life for ever. I was at a loose end and didn't know what to. By now we had been in the shop for eight years, the war was still in full swing, sweets were rationed, clothes were rationed, and food was rationed, I can't think of anything that wasn't rationed, except school.

. Dad seemed to know a few people who knew a few people that helped keep us supplied with 'things', I never knew where 'things' came from, but at that age I didn't know much anyway. Mother told us how to make butter and cheese from milk; as we lived near a farm and had access to surplus dairy products that would otherwise have been thrown away we always seemed to have some spare milk. She could make a good sausage pie out of the stuff that came in cans. I never did stomach dried eggs though we were able to get fresh ones from the farm on occasion.

It was now that Mum & Dad sprung the news that we were going to have a new brother or sister and would have to leave the shop, as Mum couldn't manage the house and a new baby as well as my big sister and me.

All dressed up for a night out.

CHAPTER 3 NEW HOUSE, SCHOOL, NEW EVERYTHING

We sold the shop and moved quite a few miles down the same road to a terraced house, still with only two bedrooms, but this time there was a wash basin and bath over the stairs between the two bedrooms. The toilet was still outside at the top of the yard, there was a bit of a garden in the back yard. Dad had a plot of land across the path at the back which eventually became space for a garage, this was overlooked by the Bell field, why it was called The Bell Field we never found out, the field belonged to the local farmer and had a pond which we used to swim in and share with the cows.

There were two main rooms, the front was very tiny and you could just about get a three piece suite in with coffee table, when we got a telephone it sat on the windowsill and next to it Mother used to have some cactus. No guesses as to who sat on them whilst taking a phone call. I can still feel the prickles. The back room was big enough to use as a lounge/dining room and when we had family parties, which we did quite often, we would open the table and extend it with the sewing machine table so that we could all get round it. There was an open fire with an oven at the side, not one of you black lead types, but a modern stove enamel one. You could make some lovely casseroles, baked slowly in the oven and sitting on the kerb with your back to the oven was bliss in winter.

Dad also had an allotment across the road; this meant once again we had fresh vegetables even grapes for this time he also had a greenhouse, which was his pride and joy. There was a little pantry added to the kitchen, which was eventually made into a toilet. At last Mother had what she had always wanted, in inside loo. Brenda, who by now was 15 yrs and nearly out of school, she stayed at the original high school but I was transferred to the nearby Grammar School where I took English, Maths, Science, French & Latin not German & Domestic Science as Brenda had done. I know it sounds awful but I vowed if ever I had children I would treat them as individuals and not as part of the same mould. We weren't really catty or jealous, just different.

Still I wanted to dance but where to go was the problem as the teachers were nearly all of an age whereby they were called up into the forces. We found a dancing school that happened to be nearer our old house than the new one. It was over the co-op, (why do all dance studios seem to be above the co-op?) you would never know it was there unless someone told you. It was very popular every one knew Eddy Cooke's, I went twice a week with my dancing shoes in a little fabric bag like a dolly bag, after I had done my homework, My Mother told me," Do your homework as soon as you got home so that you have more time after tea to do what you want". She was very good at making suggestions.

This time it wasn't tap or ballet but ballroom dancing and I had to learn a completely new technique, a new way with my feet and arms, my feet were no longer allowed to be at ten to two, or with the toes turned out, I had to walk with toes pointing straight forward. My arms had no set positions as in ballet but strictly held in position with my partner. That was another thing; I could no longer dance on my own but needed a partner, **a boy,** whatever next.

I spent ages in front of a mirror training my arms and feet into the right positions. Eventually I got so that I could walk with my toes pointing straight forward, I could still do the splits and tie myself in knots, lie on my tummy on the floor and touch the top of my head with my toes, but this wasn't much good for ballroom dancing. It kept me supple though.

I went to church over the hill and became a member of the youth club. We formed a concert party and gave concerts to the old people's homes and orphanages we were a happy band of youngsters, doing everything together, going on outings on our bikes. I even had a boy friend or two; one was so serious he said he would throw himself in the canal when I dumped him. I said I would hold his coat if he did. I never heard from him again. Wet blanket that he was. Mother told me" You can manage without a fella any day", and I believed her – then.

In the concert party we did sketches that one of the boys had written, mainly cribbed from the radio, sang songs individually or as a chorus One or two of the boys played instruments, one saxophone, one piano and one drums, quite a band, we thought they were super, they accompanied us with their music, and I danced, of course though I could sing as well, we formed a chorus with some of the others who liked to dance too. Having had experience of performing on the stage during my ballet career I was given the job of choreographer and sometimes producer depending on the type of act we were performing. It was all very amateurish but good fun and the people we used to entertain seemed to like it, or were they just being polite? Things have changed so much that these days we would have been laughed off the stage.

We put on a pantomime Cinderella, which was written by us all, everyone contributing something. I played Cinderella and my friend from Grammar school, Mavis Lees played Prince Charming. The boys were the ugly sisters and a good time was had by all. Mother made some of the costumes. We played to full houses every night. The profits went to keeping the youth club running.

The cricket club belonging to the church needed a scorer so not one to refuse a challenge I said I would do it. From then on cricket became another of my passions. Not only did I score but took up the bat and learned how to play the game I could never bowl for toffee. So what with rehearsals, dancing classes, the concert party and cricket not to mention school and homework. I was kept pretty busy until the arrival of our little sister. One Saturday in November she wasn't there, on Sunday morning she was, she was to be called Cynthia, The days changed for me after that.

Mother never was one for exercise; I know she once wore a swimming costume but like the song her bathing suit never got wet, I know because there is a picture of her wearing it, but I bet it got lost sometime in a move. She did on occasion play tennis but only because Dad joined a tennis club as he enjoyed playing so much. He loved to play doubles with Aunt Agnes, his younger sister. My Mother told me she had had ST Vitus Dance when she was little and this left her a bit unpredictable, she had her good days and her bad ones. When it was a good day Dad used to play with her at the back of the court as she hit the ball so hard and got nearly everything back over the net. But when it was a bad day the rolls were reversed and Dad had to do the running at the back of the court, Aunt Agnes was at the net where he could keep an eye on her, nothing much went past her as she was much taller than Dad. Mother sat on the side lines cheering him on and her love for tennis lasted all her life even to writing down all the winners of Wimbledon in a book every year.

Even though Mother was an excellent cook, she still liked the shop bought cream cakes, especially cream crisps as they were made from puff pastry, a thing she had never mastered. Also she loved meringues oozing with cream, she told me she only had to look at cream or chocolate and she put on weight. In spite of this disadvantage every Saturday I pushed my little sister along to the bakery to stock up on bread and cakes, Mother loved her cakes Dad worked there on a part time basis to make a bit extra cash. Every Friday night he used to help his friend, who owned the shop, bake the bread ready for the Saturday rush. There is nothing like the smell of freshly baked bread, the trouble is you eat too much oozing with butter, He was pooped Saturday morning and slept through till it was time for him to go to the football match; this didn't last long as it was very hard work trying to do his day job as well. By now he was Superintendent at the Insurance Company he worked for.

Mother liked to have the house full of youngsters, we had some in most nights and she was kept busy baking for them. Even though things were still rationed she managed to make all sorts of goodies. We used to have huge birthday parties. I remember one in particular. Dad liked to tease and his favourite party game was 'silent band'. If you don't know it, one person is sent out of the room, when they come back in they play an instrument without making any sound and the rest of the gang have to guess what it is. Simple but in those days, good fun. One of my friends was very gullible and when Dad suggested he came as a one man band, can you imagine the fun we had. Gentle fun, not pulling him to pieces just laughing with him at the antics he went through trying to get us to guess what he was playing.

One pancake day, the house was full, as usual of our friends, mainly boys; Dad was in one of his teasing moods. He and Mother were in the kitchen making a stack of pancakes for the gang and we were sat around forks ready to eat them. They duly arrived and Dad carefully handed the plates of steaming pancakes to everyone. He stood back with a grin on his face; I knew he was up to something, but what? We soon found out. Two of the boys had great difficulty in cutting their pancakes; Dad had put a strip of gauze in them. He doubled up laughing; Mother hit him across the shoulders saying, "Oh, Harold, you are a one". Never a dull moment with Dad & Mum around.

Every Wednesday night Mum & Dad went to Oldham Rep to see whatever plays was on that particular week. We of course filled the house with our gang and made the most unholy row. Ken Baldwin would play the piano and the rest of the gang got out the pots and pans to make a tympani orchestra. We rolled back the carpet as the floor was tiled so we could dance and sing all night, what the neighbours must have thought we never knew for they didn't complain, not once. Cynthia on the other hand complained if we stopped, she couldn't get to sleep if it was quite.

So all in all I was kept pretty busy one way and another, but it didn't stop me dancing. I took my silver medal exam and passed highly commended, my teacher partnering me, later I took the gold medal with the same result. After that came the gold medal with bar, I loved it and felt that my feet hardly touched the floor when the music started. By now I had a partner who did all the practice with me and we entered a few competitions just for the fun of it. He was called Terry and was quite a bit taller than me, then who wasn't? Terry looked good in white tie and tails; we made a reasonably handsome couple and danced well together. Dad called him the chinless wonder as he did have a slightly receding lower jaw; it made no difference to his dancing feet.

Mum & Dad had some friends who lived nearby and we got to be close friends even going to stay with Eric's father in Llangollen for a holiday. It was lovely there we could walk along the canal and see chaffinches, something I had never seen before. Eric and Muriel were the ones who we went to the Town Hall dances with. Eric seemed to know a 'lot of people'

Mother made my dresses not all covered in sequins as they are now as the war was still going on and clothes were on coupons. It was a case of make do and mend, altering a dress of Mothers, you can make lovely floaty dresses when the material is cut on the cross. And of course Mother begged material from Grandma who seemed to have a huge 'rag bag' I remember one on particular; it was white moss crepe with a cape and trimmed with black sequins. Long of course, it hung beautifully and twirled a treat. Mother always turned out something special.

My partner and I not only entered competitions where we did reasonably well, but we did a few demonstrations, which I loved, he was a great dancer but not a qualified teacher as I was. It made no difference; we got on well together and soon got to know each others movements, it was if the music flowed with each step

The war ended and once again I found myself in Blackpool, this time as a fifteen year old young lady on holiday with a few friends, parents these days couldn't let a group of 15 yr olds go away unsupervised, it just wouldn't be safe. I met lots of boys who were still in the army, navy or air force and went dancing in the Tower ballroom. Life was fun once again even though things were still rationed

We had to take our ration books with us even on our holidays. It was funny there I was in Blackpool just as I had been at the beginning of the war. Full Circle. The promenade was full of soldiers, airmen and sailors of every description; they seemed to congregate on Blackpool for their leave. We had a great time playing games on the beach and dancing in the tower ballroom. We, that is some of my friends and I, went dancing at The Hill St., Stores where I met a young soldier, he was stationed nearby and was an excellent dancer. Unfortunately his home was Welwyn-

Garden-City which meant we hardly saw one another. His style of dancing was far advanced from mine as he learned to dance in London. I travelled to and fro to Welwyn on the odd occasion when I had the train fare and he and I danced at The Locarno in London, I thought it wonderful and very grown up. I could go back to my dancing school and tell them all about it. Our partnership didn't last all that long, but it broke my heart when he broke it off. Ah! Young love how hard it can be Dad thought me a silly little girl, why is it that at that age everything seems to be so important? The end of the world on a big scale, ah me!

I persuaded Mum & Dad to let me leave school to study for my teacher's exam in Ballroom dancing. It took some persuading but in the end I got my way and became the youngest teacher in England passing the exam highly distinguished, thrilled to bits. I was so pleased and couldn't wait to start teaching, then got a job teaching at night school where the pupils were all older than me, we all enjoyed the evening classes and though I only did it for a year or two it gave me a good lot of experience in teaching all manner of people. I was thrilled to bits, doing what I wanted to do and enjoying every minute, not many people are so lucky.

Apart from teaching I had to get a 'proper job' it wasn't selling baby ribbon at Woolworth's which was what Father said I would end up doing. At first I went as trainee chemist but soon found the hours didn't fit in with the rest if my activities, so then I got a job as a yarn tester in the local cotton mill, which was quite interesting testing the strength of the cotton. Measuring the staple length, trying out new cotton on the trial ring spinning frames, each day was different and interesting. I had to check the humidity of the ring room every morning and afternoon to make sure it was humid enough to spin the yarn unbroken, which is mainly why the North of England was chosen as the best place to spin cotton.

I also went to night school taking a course in conversational French and Psychology, both of which were very interesting, I loved the French but the psychology was a little hard. Time was passing by very nicely, by now I was seventeen, nearly eighteen and of course I knew everything there was to know, as you do at that age, dancing and work and cricket taking up most of my time. The Cotton mills in the town and around and about Oldham decided to hold a Cotton Queen competition, the mill I worked for put my name forward as their entrant. Once again Mother made my dress, no coupons by now thank goodness. I found out later that the girl who won had had her dress made professionally and more or less had her name engraved on the trophy before it began My first lesson in who you know not what you know or who you are, Mother said I was too good for that lot, "Chin up, my girl" My dress was a fitted Empire style which 'twizzed' very nicely, that was always the criteria for a dance dress for me, it had to twizz, or float, if it didn't it was no good to dance in. Coming second didn't bother me as Terry was there and we danced the night away. I got a big bouquet which I took home to Mother; she was as pleased as punch. The competition happened the week before my 18th birthday, everything happened that weekend.

Friday night was the competition; Saturday night was a different thing entirely.

Chapter 4 BLIND DATE.

Brenda was courting a boy from our gang of friends, I had been to Grammar School with him, he was in the army and stationed in Chester. He asked his friend to come up to play tennis and asked me to make a foursome up at a dance that evening at the Town Hall, of course I said yes. This was one time when Brenda didn't say 'If our Madge is coming, I'm not'.

It was Saturday and as usual I was scoring at the local cricket ground, I knew this boy was coming with my Brenda and her boyfriend. What had I let myself in for when I said I would make up the foursome? Whoever goes on a blind date? I DO, I must be mad. I was late getting home and went through the Camp Field where the army had been stationed during the First World War and across the Bell Field past the pond and cows, and must have looked as though I had been dragged through the proverbiable hedge backwards. When I finally got home and walked down the yard into the house there was this person sat on a dining chair in the middle of the room smoking a pipe. 'Must be intellectual if he's smoking a pipe', I thought. He looked at me and said 'Hello', I said 'Hello' back then we had tea. He was tall, about 6ft, and as I am only 5ft.2ins. That was TALL. His hair was light brown and wavy, not short as I had expected him being in the army. He was as I said smoking a pipe, Dad had smoked a pipe occasionally but it made him cough, so he didn't do it any more, but this boy did and looked good doing it. He was wearing a tweed jacket, I say it was green but as he is a bit colour blind I doubt he will agree to that. Oh! And he had light blue eyes. Deep sigh.

This is a picture of him in his uniform, I never did actually see him in it, and he was always in civvies when we met. He was in The Royal Engineers and became a Corporal.

Later when the dishes were all washed and put away, I disappeared to get changed, boy did I get changed. Instead of the brown woollen stockings which I sometimes wore to cricket when it was cold, I dug out my best nylons; they were scarce still, even so long after the war. Sweets were still rationed, it went on for ages.

I had just acquired a dress in the 'new look' style, it was white with lozenges in jewel colours and three black bands of gross grain with a bow on each band on the left side the skirt which reached mid calf. All the rage, the New Look from Paris since clothes had come off rationing. Then to finish the effect, white stiletto heeled shoes in buckskin, this plus my make up finished the transformation. I never had any trouble with my hair, I guess I was lucky as it is naturally curly and fair (with a little help these days), all I have to do is wash it and run a comb through it and it looks O.K. Except when I was doing a demo. or competition, then I went to the hair dressers for some exotic design even had it coloured purple once and green and yellow. The youngsters today think they invented fashion. Getting ready never did take me a long time, so there I was back in the dining/lounge room ready for action.

We were going to the Town Hall for a dance. I soon found out he couldn't dance and no matter how long or how many times I tried, I never could teach him to waltz, he always put or tried to put four beats where there should only be three. It didn't seem to matter though; we had other things on our minds. We got on fine talking about cricket; I don't think he knew of any other girl who had a pin up of a cricketer in their office, usually they were film star mad, I never was.

As I said before he was in the army, stationed at Chester with Brenda's then boy friend, now husband, and got home most weekends so we made arrangement for the next week, which was by the way, my 18th birthday,

I couldn't wait for the day to come when I would see 'this boy' again. His name was Ken; Brenda's boy friend was also called Ken, which made for a lot of confusion. "Which Ken, your Ken or my Ken?' In the end we settled for Ken B (my Ken) and Ken Briggs (her Ken) both their surnames began with B which made things even more difficult.

He arrived mid afternoon, I forsook cricket for one Saturday, and he had brought me a lovely pair of pale blue kid leather gloves for my birthday. I forget what we did that evening, it didn't seem to matter, and we were together. I don't know if you believe in love at first sight, I think it is more love at first acquaintance. The more you get to know each other the more comfortable you are in each others company. It just seemed right for us to be an item. His birthday is twelve days later then mine two years earlier, in other words he was two years older than me. We seemed to have so

much in common that it was natural for us to be together. Whenever we could we spent time alone together on his weekends leave, we would walk along the canal towpath, arms round each other stopping every few yards for a kiss and a cuddle. He says it still makes him tingle just thinking about it. After about three weekends he asked my Father if we could get engaged,
Dad said no we hadn't known each other long enough, I can understand that now but then it was a disaster I sulked for ages but it made no difference; we just had to put up with it. Then we did what all couples in love do even though they may say they don't and tell their children not too, we made love, just the once , but that is all it takes. I became pregnant, oops!
I didn't know how to tell Mum & Dad, what would they say. Finally I told Mum on our way home from the pictures, I knew she couldn't make too much fuss if I did it in public; Mother never was one for a scene. She was very surprised, I don't know why; I was very naïve in those days, Mother never talked about IT as they do now. So I didn't know what IT was till we did IT.
What a to do, Mum & Dad blew their tops, his parents were more understanding but weren't quite happy with the situation. We would have to get married after all, three months after we first met. There was one further difficulty, we had arranged our holidays and were unable to alter them. I was going with friends to the Isle of Wight and he had leave to go to the Isle on Man with his parents. We say we spent our honeymoon ISLES apart, we never did have a real honeymoon because of the baby and because we couldn't afford it. What a way to start a marriage.

Mother and I made my wedding outfit. No fancy dress for me, a blue suit with white accessories, and my sisters were bridesmaids. Nothing went according to plan, the bouquet wasn't the one I ordered, I wanted a spray and got a big round bouquet the roses were nice though, The vicar forgot to order the organist and the carpet for the church so I clomped down the aisle instead of tripping lightly. We were having the reception at home with Mother and a few friends doing the catering. Who should arrive just before we set off for church but his Aunt Ida & Uncle George? "We've come to the Wedding" they announced and in they marched They deliberately weren't invited, for all sorts of family reasons namely that they were both a bit odd Uncle George especially. They brought a set of Apostle Tea spoons which were tarnished with age, antiques I supposed. They would keep putting them at the front of the wedding presents. Brenda kept putting them at the back. It was funny really looking back, but at the time it was a bit traumatic. We still have most of them, at first we thought they were real silver, but alas only E.P.N.S. they come in handy for boiled eggs. I can still see Brenda Tut-tutting, trying to hide them and Aunt Ida fishing them out from the back of the display and putting them right front centre of the table. We still laugh about it even now.

Each time new guests arrived, my poor Father had to run to his allotment and rob his precious carnations, which were then made into buttonholes. The carnations were some special ones that Dad had grown himself, they were lilac/grey with deep burgundy frilled edge and they smelled of cinnamon. When later, Dad died, so did the carnations and I have never been able to replace them try as I may at every Horticultural Show we have been to.

Meanwhile I was getting dressed and looked out of the window to see my future husband going to the church in the taxi. With him was Brenda's boyfriend who was best man. My husband told me later that when they were outside the church waiting for me to arrive, he was sat on a tomb stone waiting patiently smoking his pipe and my soon to be brother-in-law was pacing up and down getting very agitated. The vicar told Ken to try to calm the groom down. Ken told him he wasn't the groom but only the best man, we had a good laugh about that. Ken Briggs always gets agitated over the slightest thing whereas my Ken is as calm as can be., he takes everything in his stride, but can sometime blow his top and woe betide you if you cross him when he is in a 'moody'.

Another of his friends who was an usher managed to get into every photograph and had to be brushed out or whatever they did in those days. So what with one thing and another my wedding day didn't go according to plan, does it ever? I had always thought of myself floating down the aisle in a beautiful wedding dress with the perfect spray of flowers, not in a blue suit, clomping down with no carpet, no music and a bouquet that you could hide behind it,

Ken was still in the army but came home every weekend; I still have the letters he wrote to me mid week, his writing is as bad now as it was then so deciphering them was a bit of hit and miss, I knew what he meant though. We used to meet under the clock at Central Station, the station is no longer there, it is an exhibition hall, but the clock is still there and it works even now..

Living with his parents wasn't a bed of roses as they thought I had deliberately trapped Ken for his money. What money? I'm still looking for some. Their house was a three bed roomed terraced house in Eccles, which wouldn't have been too bad except they had a lodger who had the small bed room. I did think that with a baby on the way he would have moved out leaving us with the space. But no, he was treated like one of the family and Mother-in-law cooked all him meals, did his washing and cleaning and gave him the run of the house just as if he was their relation. He stayed there till the day he died; it was as much his house as anyone's. It made it awkward for us when the baby arrived as we had to have it in our room all the time.

There were three rooms downstairs a lounge and a dining room with a kitchen extension which had a coal fire with a boiler behind this mad it very hot in summer as you had to light the fire just to have hot water. Oh" for the Good Old Days. I did think we would have had the smallest room to ourselves, but NO we had to join in with everyone else, even the lodger.

They booked me into a private nursing home for the birth, without asking me what I wanted to do. I would have preferred to be at home. In fact I had very little to say about most things, they both thought I was too young to know anything. Mother-in-law chose the pram and the cot, (as they paid for them as a gift), they were beautiful and we were grateful for the thought and the present.

Chapter 4 EARLY MARRIED LIFE

Ken was demobbed in the October, so that meant that we were together all day and every day till he got a job, He started as a draughtsman and earned less than he did in the army, and the only good thing about living with his parents was that we didn't have to pay any rent.

Our son arrived 6 weeks early by induction. Ken's Dad always said that it would snow when the baby arrived, and it did. They all trudged up to the nursing home not quite knee deep in snow but deep enough. I don't remember much about the actual birth as I was knocked out at the time. When I finally saw him he was so small 4 ½ pounds and yellow. I was told that premature babies were sometimes born with jaundice and it was nothing to worry about. In the room next to mine was a Chinese lady and the family weren't sure whose baby was whose. He wouldn't feed properly, so they had to give him glucose for the first few times till he got used to it and his colour became more normal.

It was January and snowing, my husband was working and going to night school so coming to see us made it a long day for him, he was given permission to come to se us after night school. Thank goodness we were only there for one week; I don't think I could have stood any longer. Mother and Father came to visit bringing Cynthia, his Aunt, she is only 6 years older than him. She would keep calling him Douglas, where she got that name from I never found out. Mother had made all sorts of clothes, some knitted some sewn, he didn't want for a thing.

Home with a new baby, a mother-in-law who was inclined to take over, thinking I was too young to know about things, she forgot that I had been looking after my little sister for the past six years and was used to baby things, she even came into the bedroom when the baby was crying and took over there. Needless to say things were a bit strained between us.

We had no privacy, no room of our own, even the bedroom was on occasion taken over by mother-in-law. My husband was working, going to night school, and sometimes school on Saturday mornings, he was working so hard to try to improve our situation yet, he was also a Scout leader and would go to Camp with the Troop, and then there was cricket in the summer and rugby in the winter and occasionally tennis. Luckily his Mother had sent his golf clubs to the jumble sale when he was in the army otherwise who knows what else he would have done?

So I was left to cope under very trying circumstances. No wonder I had a row with my Mother-in-law and went home to Mother in tears, not his fault, but I couldn't cope with constantly being told what to do. Father-in-law was always right and mother-in–law always knew best. I wasn't allowed an opinion or if I expressed one it was wrong." Don't do that or you will spoil baby's temper." "You mustn't leave him crying like that". Those two were the two expressions that stick in my mind even after all the years that have since past, those and." He must have his bath every night at six o'clock or you will upset his routine". To have that nearly all day was at times more than I could stand Is it any wonder I went home to Mother?

Poor Ken he was in the middle of it all and when he came to take me home, he couldn't understand what all the fuss was about. He was not always there to see it, but when I explained he was more understanding and said he would speak to his parents about it, so I went back with him. Lot of good it did.

A year after our wedding Brenda and her Ken got married; she had a white dress, I was Matron-of-Honour, the organ, the carpet and the honeymoon. In other words, the lot. They even moved into Grandma & Granddads' house, he had died a few months before the wedding it was still furnished so they could just move straight in. I could have been jealous, but I wasn't,. I had something they never would have, I had Michael. He was gorgeous with curly hair so fair it was nearly white, so well behaved and nearly crawling I loved him to bits.

^The coronation of Queen Elizabeth was a big occasion not to be missed and Father bought a Television for us all to watch it on. We had a party with every one there and Mother, as usual, made masses of food for us all. I remember it rained and the picture wasn't all that good, but we watched with wonder at the new invention, Television.

Ken's Dad didn't like spending money, he thought me very extravagant, but eventually of course Ken's parents had to buy one, all their friends were talking about how marvellous Television was. Michael must have been about 3yrs. old. We had put him to bed and just settled down for a night's entertainment when a little figure dressed in his pyjamas blonde curls slightly awry, sidled into the lounge. He stood there for a while holding the door handle, eyes glued onto the T.V. then he slid in between Ken & me we just looked at each other and smiled to ourselves. After about 5 minutes a little voice piped up. "I just came down for a drink of water" We had to laugh, and then picked him up and took him back to bed.

Still, I survived until my 21st birthday. His parents would never baby sit for us even though they were in the same house so when we asked if they would look after Michael whilst we went out for my birthday, guess what? , they said "No". So Ken & I had a blazing row and I ended up going to the pictures on my own. Some birthday.

Mother and Father did come down a few days later with Cynthia and we had a bit of a party, but it wasn't the same somehow. Another milestone of how things never turn out the way you imagine. Mother said "It's no good moaning to me, I can't do anything about it, and you'll just have to get on with it".

I tried to get some part time work, as mother-in-law didn't mind looking after Michael through the day; in fact she enjoyed it, taking him round to show to her friends. All I could get was working in a cake shop, but it helped a bit with the money situation. You may have noticed that dancing is never mentioned now. "Now you have a family, you have no time for fancy things like dancing. It isn't proper work for a mother is it? So with no encouragement and not much time dancing had to go on hold.

I did produce the scout shows and pantomimes as well as helping write them. They seemed to go down well with the family and friends of the scouts and cubs. Everyone enjoyed them and threw themselves into the production and making scenery and costumes. It was a real joint effort and well worth it. It helped satisfy my dream. I loved the theatre and anything connected to it.

We lived with his parents till Michael was 4 yrs old and nearly ready for school. Then Eric a friend of Fathers' had a small two-up two-down to rent and we accepted gladly. You walked straight into the front room which we furnished with a second hand three piece suit and one or two knick knacks.. The kitchen had a flag floor which was cold in the winter; there was a coal fire with the usual back boiler, hot in summer but O.K. in the winter months. The stairs went up from the kitchen into a little landing, the front bed room wasn't too bad but the back was tiny. The bed was nearly like a bunk bed being placed over the stairs, there was room for a chest of drawers and that was it.. The toilet was, of course, way out back across the yard. Keeps you fit running there in winter. The move was planned, all the arrangements had been made, removal van all sorted out., then whammy - Ken was rushed to hospital with kidney stones, they were so bad he nearly lost his kidney and ended up with a scar the whole length of his abdomen. Like a zip fastener. This was during the move to the little house, I needed help.

Luckily one of his friends from the scouts supplied the muscle and helped me with everything, together with my father & mother and some friends. We managed the move as well as visiting Ken in hospital. It was a bit hectic but we did it and Ken finally came home to a reasonably tidy house. Most of our things were second hand, which isn't how newly weds like to do things these days.

When I first moved into Ken's parent's house they didn't have a washing machine, just the old fashioned dolly tub and washing board with a wooden mangle. Mother-in-Law had to get up very early to get the boiler going. When I mentioned getting a washing machine as we had at home I was told in no uncertain tone" They didn't wash as clean as the dolly tub did." When I replied" Well, my clothes must be very dirty then". The conversation was quickly changed to another subject. So, one of the first things I saved up for was a washing machine.

Ken's Father had an opinion on everything and if yours differed in any way you were wrong. He wouldn't buy a fridge freezer because you could taste the freezer. When I asked why he liked ice cream, once again the subject was changed, that is an entirely different matter. My Mother never could understand him.

The washing machine I bought was a very old one with a hole in the tub, which I mended with a pot mender. One of those things we did during the war to make your pans last longer. It worked for a while and I felt quite liberated

We stayed in that house for twelve months, and then Ken's dad gave us the deposit for a house. We couldn't choose the house we wanted but had to have the one he said he liked, because it had a nice view from the lounge window. I know I shouldn't be so ungrateful as they were very good at helping us out, it was the way they did it. Always treating Ken as a little boy who couldn't look after himself without their help. He knows what I mean and just laughs about it even now, he says they always treated him as if he was still seven, it's a good job he can laugh about it, but then that's Ken all over.

Chapter 5   All SPORT AND SCOUTING

The new house was once again small, after the large rooms at Mum & Dad's I felt hemmed in by the smallness of them. I wanted to knock the wall down between the dining room and the lounge to make one good sized room, but Ken was afraid the whole house would fall down if we did that, so he said "No". There was a hall with the stairs going up to a landing then a turn to the bed rooms, and, a BATHROOM. 3 bed rooms, two of which were a reasonable size but the third one was a box room with the stairs partly invading into the room. It would hold a single bed a wardrobe and not much else.
The kitchen was so small you could touch every piece of furniture without stretching. No room for a washer even if I had one, which I didn't, yet. There were three doors in the kitchen, one to the hall and one leading outside and a third one which was divided into two. The top half had a stone shelf like the old fashioned larder type, on which we kept a minute fridge, the smallest you could get. The bottom half opened to the coal bunker, this had a door outside so that you could load it up after the coalman had dumped it on the drive.
The view Ken's Father raved about was overlooking some spare ground covered in weeds etc. and the main road, in the far distance were some hills. "You can see for miles" he said. The window frames were metal, all rusty, they took some scraping and sanding down to get then ready for painting, as Ken is allergic to enamel paint, guess who used to do the painting?

Under the floor boards, we later found out, was three feet of water, which was missed in the survey, we had to get the fire service to pump it out on more than one occasion.

Michael started to go to school, it was about three miles from home and therefore too far to walk so I had to take him on the bus everyday and pick him up after school had finished, He enjoyed the lessons but didn't much care for school dinners, what child did in those days. After a while he became good at going to school on his own, there were a few other children who went on the same bus every day. One day someone told me that he had fallen off the bus just as it approached the bus stop. Luckily he had rolled away and came to no harm, but he didn't say anything to us and when I asked him about it he just shrugged his shoulders and said it wasn't worth saying anything, as he wasn't hurt. Typical Michael, don't speak unless necessary. He kept going to the same school until he reached 11 yrs; all along his progress was good and steady, just what we expected from Michael. get on with things without making a fuss - that is unless a fuss is needed. He must have heard what mother told me.

Ken went to work on his trusty bike, the one he used to cycle to see me on at weekends when he was still in the army. He had had it for ages; thank goodness the traffic wasn't as bad as it is in these days. We got along, I won't say nicely as the money was tight, as usual. We even had a burglary, the one time we didn't have a dog, the police were surprised when we told them the only money that was stolen was 2/6p (12 1/2p in today's money) That was all I had left to see me through to the end of the week. Ken had to go to our friends up the street to borrow some money to go to work with. Ken, bless him, was content as long as he had two pennies to rub together, he left managing the household accounts to me along with everything else, like decorating, doing the garden, anything mechanical or electrical, cooking and cleaning. Oh! I forgot the washing. Washing cricket whites along with muddy rugby tackle in the winter Washing, the bane of my life, that and ironing.

Ken was quite happy playing cricket in the summer and rugby in the winter with a little tennis in between He became captain of the second team at cricket which as well as keeping wicket and opening the batting, kept him pretty busy every Saturday and some Sundays, there were even mid week matches and committee meetings. Not much time for 'doing things around the house'. All those cricket whites to wash; I did a lot of dancing in the bath to get them white, still not having a washing machine. I used to leave them soaking over night, then drain off the water and fill the bath with hot soapy water, take off my shoes and stockings and dance on them The only dancing I did those days. Then I had to wring them by hand before taking them downstairs to peg on the line, wet days were a night mare, I had to go to the laundrette.

Michael was taking an interest in the game as well and I spent a lot of time in the back garden teaching him the basics, my bowling wasn't up to much, it never had been. He used to have a ball in a sock suspended from a rope hung from the garage door when we got one, and spent ages hitting it. Clunk – clunk – clunk, nearly all day long. Very soporific if it didn't get on your nerves.

When Michael was five we went to Butlins with Mother, Father and Cynthia who was by now 11 yrs. They were more like brother and sister than Aunt and Nephew as there was only 6 years between them we had a fine old time at Butlins doing all the things that were available to us. We had gone in Dad's car which was a bit of a squeeze but as usual we managed.

There was one time when Michael decided he wanted to roller skate, Dad said he would go with him, but Michael in his typical way said "NO, I can do it." However Dad went into the skating rink with him and for his sins got his shins kicked till they were black and blue. Bless him he never complained, he enjoyed being with his only Grandson. Butlins didn't suit Mother, she was far to fussy about her food and having two sitting in the dining room were a horror, she had to make sure everything was clean before she would even sit at the table, and the foods she didn't like were on a longer list than the ones she did..

Then I became pregnant. This was the third time. The second was when we were at the in-laws. Michael was two, we didn't tell anyone to begin with, and then when I miscarried the doctor told me to go home and rest for a day or two. Did I get any sympathy? No, all I got was a lecture on birth control. The best way it seemed was total abstinence. So this time I didn't tell anyone for ages except Ken of course.

All went well till 3 months and I had another miscarriage. We were as usual broke and I needed coal for the fire, I had enough money to get to Mothers where I filled a shopping bag with coal before coming home. The weight of the bag was too great and as a result I miscarried, we had to settle for being a one-child family. There wasn't the counselling there is today; you just had to get on with it, so that's what I did, got on with it. The girl next door was expecting the same time as I was and I felt very tearful when her baby arrived, still I had Ken & Michael, what more did a girl want?

I got a job as a temp and went all over acting as a bookkeeper or secretary or filing clerk or what-ever job came along. It helped pay the bills and even went to paying for our holidays, plus it was convenient and didn't interrupt with school or housework, as a fulltime job would have done. Except once I did get a full time job when Michael was eight. I was in statistics and really enjoyed the work, the only thing I didn't like was having to rush home and do all the housework, make all the meals and try to have it ready for when Ken came home,

Michael was just the same, they both wanted everything done for them. I got little if no help. Poor little me…I got to screaming point, so I handed in my notice and went back to being broke. The other time when I was temping I was offered a job as the director's secretary at a luggage firm, which I would have loved as they supplied the luggage for the James Bond films, who knows what would have happened. I can dream can't I? Things sure have changed these days, men muck in with things Oh! For emancipation years ago. Pity I had to turn it down, it was the type of job I would have enjoyed

We usually went to Morecambe Bay Holiday camp for our annual holiday. We had been going there ever since Ken left the army. The first time we went they blew bugles for everything. When the one went for reveille Ken was out of bed like a shot. He thought he was still in the army, we had good times there, playing tennis, table tennis, snooker and all other games, Ken even played cricket. He was offered a job as professional for Heysham Cricket Club but didn't take it because of the distance he would have to travel. We didn't have a car in those days; every thing had to be got to either by train or bus. Ken could see no further than Morecambe, I tease him about it often. Basically I don't think he likes change of any sort and once an idea gets fixed in his mind he is very difficult to alter. We went to Morecambe for years and years and years.

We usually went to Ken's Mother & Father's every two weeks, it was quite a journey by bus and train but we took all the things needed for Michael when he was small. Ken's parents rarely came to see us because of the journey and time it took to get to see us. They still thought I was the girl who pressured their son into marriage, they didn't like me and I didn't much care for them. Michael and Ken were alright but, me, I couldn't do anything right. Ken's Dad liked to be the centre of attention and whatever he said was right, if your opinion differed from his you were always wrong. Mother couldn't understand him, She told me she thought he talked nonsense because he rarely finished a sentence and she couldn't understand what he said.

My neighbour, together with a friend who lived just up the road, and me, decided to join the Civil Defence. Mainly for a night out for a change and also that we could learn how to drive and it not cost us anything. My neighbour, Doris and I went into the ambulance section and Joan was in the Headquarters, Signals section. We really enjoyed ourselves especially the learning to drive bit. It was in a 15cwt Morris commercial and you had to double-declutch when changing gears, also it was wintertime and the roads were slippery with rain and ice. Good Fun, getting into and out of skids kept you on your toes.

Things were going along smoothly; money was a little better with me working. Michael was ten and preparing for his exams to go to grammar school. I was scoring for the cricket team, I refused to do teas, ugh, Michael was playing for the third eleven, and he was getting quite good and kept a lovely straight bat. I finally had a little twin tub washer, which I kept in the hall with a lace cloth on so that it looked like a side table. All was lovely till I found I was pregnant again. Michael was now ten nearly eleven.

This time I was oh! so careful and took things quietly. The baby didn't, it was every way but the right way, the specialist turned it the right way up a few times but I felt it churn round to whichever way it felt comfortable. It was due April Fool's Day you might guess. But what happened, he, for it turned out to be a boy kept me waiting - four days in labour, with the midwife saying, "You aren't in labour yet, it won't be born till next week" The after getting stuck on the pelvic ring, the cord was wrapped round his neck twice. "Don't push just yet, wait till I say go", then "**go**" – he arrived. He was Gareth Duncan, looking as though he had done four rounds with Rocky Marciano He was wick as they say, following my Father round the bedroom with his eyes. The midwife couldn't believe it; she hadn't seen a baby do that at only two hours old. He continued to be WICK all his childhood and beyond.

Father was delighted with another Grandson, Mother had as usual knitted and sewn so much that I didn't want a thing for the new baby. She stayed a few days to help me out; Ken's Mum & Dad came for an hour or two on the odd day. "What do you want another baby for? Isn't one enough?"

To add to the problem he had a wryneck, which meant we had to massage it every four hours otherwise, the Doctor said, he would have to go to hospital and have it stretched. So we, or rather, I, massaged it with olive oil every four hours and "Oh! By the way don't let him cry, it will only make it worse." I ask you? How do you stop a baby from crying? I was told I was spoiling him on more than one occasion, but what else could I do? I had to pick him up whenever he looked as if he was going to cry. As a consequence of this, he slept very little, only 4-5 hrs a day. By the time he was teething I was exhausted and would give anything just for a good nights sleep. He thrived though and was as wick as ever. So quick and very intelligent and me well I was pooped.;

Brenda was pregnant at the same time as me with her third child; the first two had been girls, it was a race to see who would give birth first. Two weeks after Gareth was born she had Wayne. As she and her Ken had spent a few years in Canada, Dad said "That sounds like one of those American film star names" He preferred good old fashioned names, Gareth was a bit too modern as well.

Ken still played cricket and Michael went with him, they enjoyed each other's company. Taking the pram to the cricket ground was a bit of a problem as we didn't have a car so had to travel by bus, which meant a folding push chair and all the paraphernalia that went with a baby, bottles, nappies (terry towelling ones) etc. etc. We struggled through and are still here to tell the tale though at the time it was a bit of a problem.

I had progressed in Civil Defence to become a Casualty Clearing Officer and had to go to college to study and take my exams. Ken's mother said she would have Gareth whilst I was away. She never had him again, he had her up at 5.0am and didn't go to sleep till midnight At home we had to put a bolt on the bed room door to stop him wandering all over the place once he could walk. He would climb over the side of his cot or shake it till the bottom fell out. He went to sleep about midnight and was awake again at 4 or 5 am. I have had all the housework done before anyone else got up. .How she thought I had managed for the past two years I do not know but manage I did, I had to there was no-one else to do it. I passed my exams and became a Civil Defence Instructor/Invigilator, which meant I could write the questions and take charge of examinations plus instruct the others in all aspects of First Aid. Part of my training was in the casualty dept., of the local hospital on Friday and Saturday nights. Very instructive what an eye opener. The people who came in for one reason or another were amazing. We never stopped for most of the night until about 2.am. Then there was a lull till morning. I was exhausted when I got home. It was good training and an experience I would never forget.

Chapter 6. AN END AND A BEGINNING

It was now that Cynthia told us she was pregnant, at 16yrs, her boyfriend Bernard was 17. Ken and I said we would adopt the baby but, no, they had to get married.

Cynthia and Bernard got married in the registry office and once again we had the reception at home. This picture is of Cynthia and Bernard on their wedding day in the back yard with Michael in the centre, Stephanie on the left and Fiona on the right,

Brenda's two girls. This time no odd relatives turned up we were all there. The weather was fine for September.

Afterwards, Mother Father Ken and I together with the boys went to Fleetwood for a long week end break. We enjoyed Fleetwood as Ken could sail his boats, Michael could play chess on the outdoor board, Mother and Father could sit on the beach and watch the world go by and I could browse round the local markets with Gareth in the pram to see what was on offer. We all usually had a good time at Fleetwood, there seemed to be so many things to see and do, the big boats going to the Isle of Man and all the fishing boats bringing in their catches.

We had only been home a few days when there was a knock on the door. Ken answered and walked in with a constable, my heart stopped. He told me that Father had died suddenly; I had to go to Mother as quickly as I could. We didn't have a car, it was too late for a bus, a taxi was out of the question, I didn't want to take Michael as it would be too upsetting for him and also he would miss school., we didn't have a telephone. All I could think of was asking the fellow next door, my friend's husband, would he take me and Gareth there. Luckily for me he did.

Father had had a cerebral haemorrhage and died more or less instantly, luckily he didn't suffer at all; he knew nothing about it, thank goodness. Bernard said he knelt at the side of the table to watch them playing cards before he went out to work in the evening, just keeled over and died. Mother was in a state of shock and no wonder, so sudden, here one minute and gone the next. Poor Mother, she hadn't had much of a life, what with one thing and another, this was the last straw. Cynthia and Bernard were with her but as they were 16yrs & 17 yrs respectively it couldn't have been much fun for them either. We had all the arrangements to make for the funeral and Aunt Clara & Uncle Ivan came along to help. I stayed as long as I could but had to get home to look after Ken & Michael, my loyalties were divided, Ken, bless him understood how I felt and took care of home as best he could.
We buried Father at the end of September; the smell of chrysants always reminds me of funerals even now. Mother wouldn't go anywhere near the graveside, if she had had her pinny on I'm sure she would have covered her face with it. The last picture I have of Dad is him holding Gareth & Wayne at Cynthia's wedding,

he looked so old and tired, yet he was only 56.yrs. The end of and era, my Mother told me how much she missed him; even his piano playing, she would have loved to have said "Do you have to. Harold?" a few more times. What a year, after all the trouble he caused before, Gareth arrived, then Wayne, then Cynthia getting married and now Father dying, there couldn't be anything else, surely. That was the end of things. Gareth and Wayne were the beginning as well as Cynthia's baby which arrived just 6 months afterwards. He was called Andrew. Father would have been so pleased with all these boys. Up to now there were only Brenda's two girls and Michael.

I went up to see Mother as often as I could, though this meant a trip on a bus then a train and another bus just to get there,. It took all morning then the reverse journey in the afternoon to get back home in time for Michael and tea when Ken came home from work. I usually took something for lunch, something special like cream cake or prawns. Mother was a cream cake junkie, she told me that she only had to look at cream cakes or chocolate and she put weight on. She was a big lady and always had been, she always seemed to be on a diet, not that any of them did her any good," It's in my bones" she used to say with a deep sigh. She told me that on the fair ground 'in the good old days' there was always a guess you weight man and he always guessed hers wrong, saying she was lighter than she actually was, she told me that he had said, "You must have heavy bones luv"

Michael went to the local grammar school which was next to the Sports club, he seemed to enjoy it. As I said before getting any information out of Michael was like a dentist extracting teeth. He always came home with good reports and seemed to have no trouble with exams. He was and still is very phlegmatic, just gets on with things taking things in his stride and only makes a fuss when necessary, which according to him isn't very often.

At this time the C.D. decided to hold a 'Miss Civil Defence' competition and we had heats to see who would represent Bury. I was so pleased when they decided to enter me in the competition and I won. The local paper sent a photographer round on the Monday after to take some pictures. He would come just as I had been shovelling coal into the bunker, after a quick change for both me and Gareth it was surprising how well the picture turned out.

One of my favourites in fact anyway the headline read' MOTHER WINS MISS CONTEST.' It was super Ken was so pleased.

When Gareth was two we bought our first car, Benny, a Ford with a gear stick long enough to stir a pudding, three gears and our pride and joy. We went all over in the car. I had passed my driving test and set about teaching Ken to drive. With him having had a scooter beforehand he tended to lean into the corners expecting the car to do the same. He passed his test second time after having lessons from a fiend of ours who was a police driver The double de-clutching came in useful when I had to teach Kern to drive. He had had a scooter after his trusty bike had fallen to bits, which was very useful for him going to and from work, cricket and rugby, but not much use for we four and a pram Benny took us everywhere. I tried to ride it but kept falling off and couldn't manage the pre-select gears, so I gave up. We felt so sad when we had to leave Benny on the garage forecourt when we swapped him for a newer model.

I got an evening job as a Tupperware demonstrator and took everything in the car. It brought in some extra cash and meant I could be at home through the day to see to the house and feed everyone then Ken took over in the evenings. I could arrange it that the parties I did, didn't correspond with Ken's sports club meetings or evening matches and everything in the garden was lovely. We used to go to a Holiday Camp in Morecambe as I have said before and now we took Gareth as well Michael and Gareth had a rare old time on the beach, considering the age difference they got on very well together. Michael is such an easy going type of person but woe betides you if you get on his wrong side. Gareth was by this time 3yrs old and Michael 13. Mother used to come with us for a change and we had a rare old time on the beach making pies and eating ice cream.

Cynthia's husband Bernard was in Customs and Excise and had been transferred to Hull, by this time they had a girl, Deborah, as well as Andrew, so Mother was living on her own. She didn't much care for this as she had always had someone with her. Terrible thing is loneliness. When Gareth was four And Michael 14 Mother decided to emigrate to America with Brenda and all her family, they were Mormons, having changed religion during their stay in Canada a few years previously. Things are greener everywhere else, you know how things are? Anyway, she said she was going with Brenda. My heart sank, but she packed everything up, threw a lot of things away, Then off they went., leaving Me on my own, with Ken and the boys She sold her house and in the process threw a lot of picture away without even asking did I want any, she was always tidying up and if it was in the way she threw it out without any thought as to if it was needed or not. If it didn't fit in the suitcase out it went. Eventually she and the rest of the gang went across the Atlantic to live where the grass may be greener. This was another end of an era and I was left on my own that is apart from Ken whom I adored, Michael who was growing up fast, and Gareth who by now was ready for primary school.

Heaven help the teachers.

.

Mrs. Brawn, winner of the "Miss Civil Defence" contest, is pictured at home with her younger son.

This is Ken's favourite picture taken after I had shovelled in all the coal.

Mother wins Miss C.D. contest

MORE than 600 dancers whistled and cheered when it was announced that Mrs. Madge Brawn, a 30 years old mother of two boys, had been judged the winner of Bury's "Miss Civil Defence" contest at the Prince's Ballroom on Friday. Mrs. Brawn normally spends her spare time in the uniform of a Civil Defence instructor of first aid.

There was also a fancy dress competition and Mrs. Brawn was wearing a "For Love or Money" outfit when she was awarded the Miss Civil Defence title.

She competed against 34 other girls from Civil Defence units throughout the North West. And the judges, Alderman W. K. Heaton, F. Aspinall, Fire Chief, Mr. J E. Andrew and the Director of Education, Mr. F. Dawson, had no hesitation awarding Mrs. Brawn the first prize.

The function was organised by Bury Civil Defence as the climax of a three-week recruiting drive.

"It was a great success from every angle," said the local Civil Defence chief, Mr. Walter Groom. "We recruited 125 new members bringing our total strength to 400."

The Mayor of Bury, Councillor P. Manners, who was accompanied by the Mayoress, placed the sash of honour on Mrs. Brawn, mother of an 11 years old son and a 17 months old baby boy.

In the fancy dress competition Civil Defence members disguised themselves in costumes ranging from a witch (complete with broomstick) to the mischievous Girls of "St. Trinian's." But the prize for the most original costume went to Eric Johns. The theme of his costume was "Civil Defence Headquarters," which included various signals and signs associated with the organisation—he even had a flashing light on his head!

Chapter 7 THE ADOLESCENT YEARS.

Gareth duly went off to school, leaving me at somewhat of a loose end, I had had to keep and eye on him 24-7 as they say these days. He used to climb over the garden wall and disappear up the hill and wander all over the estate. People got to know him and bring him back, much to his annoyance, he hated restrictions of any kind. Anyway he went to school and it wasn't long before he was in trouble. This picture shows Gareth between Andrew and Deborah. The Headmaster arrived one morning with Gareth in tow. He had been caught putting pink powder in the water at break time, instead of saying what it was he told the Headmaster that he had got it from Michael's chemistry set. Poor Head was devastated thinking the pupils had been poisoned. What it really was, was Strawberry Nesquick, he had taken it to liven up, in his mind a very dull morning drink. He was and still is a very intelligent boy, and as a consequence some things bored him if he found them too easy, so he looked for mischief to liven it up a bit or in some, cases a lot. Michael decided he wanted to play the drums, so off we trundled to Manchester to buy a drum kit, must be mad. Blue glitter it was with all the trappings. He had it in his bedroom and practiced to a tape recorder, can you imagine the noise? It wasn't too bad till he missed his sticks and they went flying all over the bed room.. Good job our neighbours were tolerant. He and two of his friends started

a group called The Road Sweepers very trendy in those days. Each of the other two played guitar and when all three came to practice Ken and I felt like going out for the night, but had to stay to give moral support. It didn't last long, thank goodness
. Mother had come back home from America after a while, she didn't like the weather, it was too hot for her and she didn't like the ants, they got into everything. The walnut tree they had in the back garden had a big spider init, they said it was a tarantula, but I don't know about that. So she came home and went to live with Cynthia in Hull..

They had been transferred to Manchester Airport as Cynthia was working for Service Air and both she and Bernard were on shifts, this made it easier for them for Mother to look after Andrew and Deborah whilst they both worked. She did all the cooking and cleaning and took the children to school, Cynthia had to work hard to keep up with the house, they needed a four bed roomed house with all of them. It worked out nicely for everyone.

By the time Gareth was eight Michael had taken and passed his O Level & A Level exams with flying colours and was waiting for notification of a University place. He wanted to do sport if possible, but the days went by and nothing came from the Clearing House. We went to the school and the head master told us that Michael had not passed any of his exams, this we knew was untrue. When we pointed out to Mr Sawtell that they had Michael's name spelt wrong he didn't even bother to apologise, but we afterwards found out that he had not given Michael a good report to the Clearing house and therefore Michael could not expect a place in any

University all this after Michael had taken O level and A level Economics in twelve months, he worked darned hard to get them. Ken played h--- about it and wrote to everyone he could think of to explain what had happened, then he asked at work if there was anything going there, and luckily there was a place in marketing which suited Michael a treat so instead of university he started work. He liked the getting paid bit, and when he had been there a few weeks the University places began to arrive, he had to decide what he wanted to do, the money won, he also went to school on a sandwich course and took further exams finishing up with more letters behind his name than in it. He really is a very clever boy, a bit of an absent minded professor, but very clever with it.

I had got a job as the receptionist to our own Dr .going to work for the morning and evening .surgery we had a big patient list and I really enjoyed the work, it was something I could do well and like the job at the same time. We used to get all sorts of patients some of which were from the Hospital across the road. where they catered for Drug addicts and alcoholics. There was never a dull moment, especially first thing in the morning when they came in saying they had lost their prescription, or the dog had eaten it or it got thrown away with the decorating, and could they please have another script for methadone. Never a dull moment.

Dr.Kay worked very hard in his practice and as a result had a heart attack and we had to have some Doctors who were just out of training in Hospital. They were still learning the tricks of the trade and kept going to see one of the young patients who had chicken pox, I said " You have no need to see a chicken pox case every day unless there are complications". One of them replied, "We have never seen anybody with chicken pox and so want to see how it develops". You don't think of Doctors never having seen chicken pox do you? After all we all seem to get it when we are young, but I suppose you don't think how it develops; you just want to get rid of it.

Then there was the time when Dr. Kay had a second heart attack, we got an eighty year old gentleman, who didn't do night calls, can you blame him? He came to work in a wing collar and looked very old time Victorian, a real gentleman through and through. Eventually Dr.Kay died of a third attack and I was out of a job I loved.

It had been good fun, going to work in the mini we had bought for me which was like driving in a freezer in the middle of winter and a hot box in the summer, still it got me places and was cheap enough to run. The maintenance took a lot of trouble as the engine was all cramped up. By this time I had taken up mechanics. Although Ken was in the Engineers anything mechanical seemed to break down if he tried to mend it. And according to him "These new fangled things get me all flummoxed"

After a while I decided to become a member of Bury Amateur Dramatics and stayed with them for a few years until the Director went to teach at another school. Some of the members were teachers, During my time there played the lead in 'Sailor Beware' and when I made my very first entrance a little voice called from the audience "That's my Mum" I could have crowned him, but the audience just laughed and it passed off nicely. We also did Fanny by Gaslight whilst I was there and I played the haughty maid with a cockney accent and somehow got away with it.

It was time for Michael's 21st birthday party which we held at The Sports Club with 200 invited guests and numerous others who decided to come and wish him Happy Birthday. Mother, Cynthia and I did the catering making what we could do in advance and sticking it in the freezer. The rest was made in a mad dash on the day. Mother made her famous sponge cakes which she filled with jam and cream and dusted it in icing sugar, Cut into squares it looked and tasted yummy. I can't remember what else we had apart from sandwiches and pies of all flavours. I made the cake and decorated it with sporting figures, all the sports Michael did. A good time was had by all and we were pleased when it was over, a great success.

When Gareth was 11yrs old Michael was sent to Nairobi by his employers, it was the same time that Gareth went to the new Comprehensive school that had been built nearby. His age group were the first pupils to attend a huge school and so very few

pupils. It was just like a building site, mud all around. He seemed to bring most of it home with him, but that is what boys do, isn't it? This picture of Ken was taken when he was so much like Eric Morecambe that Gareth's friends at school; asked "Why are you called Brawn when you Father is called Morecambe?"

Michael did well in Nairobi, he seemed to be enjoying every minute. His letters were few and far between, he said he didn't have much time for writing. What with playing cricket, of course and playing rugby, of course. He was the only European to play cricket for East Africa and finished up coaching the junior side, he was and still is a superb batsman. One season he scored as many runs playing Saturdays and some Sundays as the County Cricketers did in a season. He won the catching cup for our local team on more than one occasion. Mind you he still couldn't equal Ken's achievement of 9 victims in a match as wicket keeper. 8 catches and 1 stumping. Their names both appear on the Catching Cup.

He stayed in Nairobi for 2 years and then came home for a month before going back again.. We had a going away party for him which is still talked about even now, Gareth remembers it well. We had people standing all over the house and sitting on the stairs, they overflowed into the bathroom, which made it difficult on occasions. I just kept cooking rice and spaghetti till everyone was full. He went to Texas on Cricket and rugby tour during his stay playing for the Impala. One time playing rugby he broke his arm rather badly and needed plates in it for a year. He still bears the scar down his arm to his wrist. He loved Nairobi and has been back on holiday, but of course things have changed.

We still visited Ken's parents, but by car now that we had one, you still had to be careful what you said because everything came back to money. They always thought we were asking for money no matter what we said,. "You would have more money if you both stopped smoking. If you stopped smoking you would be able to afford a better car." That sort of thing, then when we went on holiday they always gave Ken spending money, they treated him as if he were still 7 yrs..old, good job we could laugh about it and even tease them on a good day.

Once again I got fed up of not doing anything and not going anywhere so I went to night school and took a course in Flower Arranging, I really enjoyed it and could have taken my City & Guilds but the cost was too much so I packed it in after 2 years. When Gareth was 14, Michael phoned and asked if he would like to go to Kenya for his summer holidays, of course he said 'yes, when can I come'. We had to get things arranged pretty quickly and all the rest of the family coughed up with some spending money for him. I ask you, how many young men of 24 would ask for their younger brother aged 14 to spend a few weeks with him? I think Michael was a bit home sick and didn't like to admit it.

Cynthia and Bernard had already been for a holiday as Cynthia was working

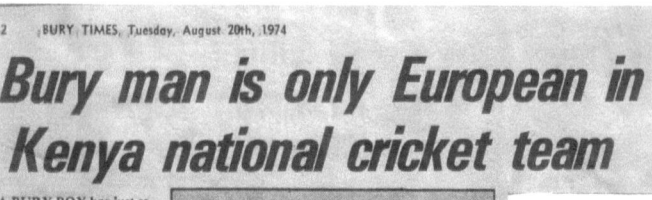

at Manchester Air Port and could get cheap flights for her family, but no one else.

Off he went what an adventure for someone his age to go all that way on their own, then he always was an independent soul. He had a whale of a time, playing cricket with Michael and the rest of the Kenya team. He was by now turning out to be a very fine fast left arm bowler. I think you can tell that I am very proud of my boys, and that includes Ken's prowess on the cricket field. Gareth went to all the places Michael could take him, down to the beach at Mombassa where he found a little emerald in the sand. I still have it to it to this day. Some things you don't throw away.

During all these years Ken had been scouting, a passion of his since he joined the cub scouts at 8yrs old. Whilst he was Scout Master at the local church we used to put on Gang Shows and pantomimes, they roped me in to do the producing and in some cases writing the script. The audience seemed to enjoy them I suppose it was mainly because their children were in it. When we were doing Aladdin we came to the very dramatic scene of Aladdin in the cave. We had the lights dimmed and at the critical moment there was a flash. A little voice piped up from the auditorium, "That's my Dad's Flash camera" Don't your children let you down when you least expect it|?

Ken gradually worked his way to District Commissioner and we both were very pleased and proud.. It made a lot of extra work as more nights and week ends were taken up with his activities, not to mention clean uniforms etc.

He was asked at one time to be assistant County Commissioner but decided against it as it would have taken all his spare time and left none for his other passions, cricket and rugby. He still played rugby, retiring when he had concussion for the third time at the age of 35.

Whilst Gareth was in Nairobi Ken and I got an Invitation to a Garden Party at Buckingham Palace, tea with the Queen, no less. Ken was still in scouting when he was awarded the Medal of Merit <u>for outstanding services</u> to Scouting, and the extra reward was an invitation to the palace. It also happened to be our Silver Wedding Anniversary. How neat was that? Couldn't be better. I got a new outfit and Ken had to have morning dress. The thing is Ken looked so like Eric Morecambe when he was younger that when we arrived at the Palace most people were expecting him to do the coin in a paper bag trick. Even the Prime Minister mistook him and you don't like to tell the Prime Minister he is wrong, do you? We went down by train and changed into out gear in The Cumberland Hotel then walked to the Palace going in by the Hyde Park Gates. We walked past the tennis courts and the lake, you couldn't hear any traffic, it was like being in the countryside, and you wouldn't know you were in the middle of London. What a wonderful experience, a once in a lifetime.

It was that very hot summer and the lawn at Buckingham Palace were parched and brown in places, my feet ached and so must the Queens for as we watched her she eased her feet out of her shoes and wriggled her toes, just like you or me would. We had cucumber sandwiches and cups of tea in china cups, sat at a table with a major and his wife. Everyone was in their best bib and

② KEN BRAWN

KEN, of CIBL, who lives in Heathfield Road, Bury, was a guest at a Buckingham Palace Garden Party — in recognition of his service to Scouting.

He joined the Scout movement as a Cub 40 years ago, at the 13th Eccles (St Andrews) and continued through the Scouts, Senior Scouts, and Rover Scouts, and then became a warranted Assistant Scout Master, in 1947, continuing until he moved to Bury in 1955.

He was Senior Scout Master in the 20th Bury (1956-59), Group Scout Master in the 17th Bury (1960-65), Assistant District Commissioner, Bury (1963-65), Assistant District Commissioner, Prestwich (1966-69), and District Commissioner Prestwich (1969-76).

Now he is taking up a new appointment as ADC, Scout Fellowship in Bury, in which he will be more concerned with the adult side of Scouting, rather than training boys.

Ken received the Scout Medal of Merit in February 1973, and the Long Service Award in January, 1976.

Ken Brawn and his wife — ready for the reception.

tucker, it was a wonderful day stored in my memory banks forever. Afterwards we went back through Buckingham Palace and out through the gates with everyone wondering who you were, what an experience, back to the Cumberland Hotel to change and a Carvery dinner before going home tired out..

We followed it by a holiday in Scotland. We had started going there pony trekking for May & September. The saddles we rode in were American ones and you could sit in them all day without getting saddle sore, it was wonderful, the forest and countryside are beautiful. Even when it poured down we enjoyed the riding, the walking and everything about it. The chef at the hotel made us a cake for our Silver Wedding; we had been there so often and knew all the regulars very well. One of them used to take Gareth poaching, or so he said, they used to come back with 4-5 pike, that fed the dogs, three great Danes.

I was at that time an amateur silversmith, I even had my own stamp at Birmingham where I sent my goods to be hallmarked,. We loved to go into the mountains looking for amethyst. We went up to Lochanhead, the highest point in Scotland looking for gold, in 'them thar hills'. I did find an old hammer with my metal detector which when we took it to the museum in Dumfries, the Curator told us it had been used by the children to break up the rock for the prospectors in the olden days. I was pleased when the curator said he would put it in the exhibition with my name on as donor. I don't know if it is still there, I would be nice to fine out.

Whilst Ken played cricket I was the scorer for both the 2nd X1 and the Sunday side. This side was a super mixture of all the players and we went to lots of different grounds. Yorkshire 2ndX1 came to play frequently and both Michael and Ken gave their all for the team. We had some great times. One year when I was scoring for the 2ndX1 on Saturday in June we had such a terrific thunderstorm, the rain lashed down and I was marooned in the score box for ages. It was at the opposite side of the pitch to the pavilion, eventually one of the cricketers had to come to fetch me in the car otherwise I would have had to swim back.

When Gareth came home he had loads of tales to tell and brought back a huge amount of raw coffee, which when we roasted it in a dry pan smelled wonderful, pity we used it all up. He brought some carved wooden book ends which I still have., How many brothers of Michael's age would send for their little brother to spend the holidays with them and both enjoy it, mainly because they both enjoy cricket. Even after all these years cricket plays a big part in our lives. Michael still plays and we watch as much as the weather will allow on television.

Gareth found school a bore and as he couldn't study the subjects he wanted to, so, he left school at 16 years old, he got a job as an apprentice engineer through a friend of ours in the cricket club. It was something he could do well as he loved getting all messy and the intricate things he had to do suited him. He bought a motor bike much against our wishes; we knew how reckless he could be and were worried sick about the things that could happen to him. He was and still is so different from Michael, Michael thinks first then thinks again, before he does anything, Gareth on the other hand jumps in with both feet without any thought whatsoever and leaves it to other people to pick up the pieces.

Michael came home from Nairobi; he had grown up a lot in 5 years. Cynthia said when he first went I was in tears and told her he wasn't old enough to go as he had only just started shaving. The truth is I hate to be parted from any of my family missed him so. Anyway he came home and bought a house. He was so proud of it. It looked like a bungalow on the front but was two storeys at the back with the bathroom on a mezzanine floor. He came to our house one night after a few weeks asking if my washer still worked. When I said yes it was he brought in 3 bin liners of washing. I told him I didn't mind washing it but would not do the ironing.. I don't do ironing.

Every year since Michael has been home from Nairobi he has toured with the Kongoni Cricket team and meets up with his old friends. They start off at Arundel Castle and go round Surrey playing on some delightful grounds. Ken and I have been on the occasional tour, Ken has played for them and I have scored. It so nice for Michael to keep up with people he met so long ago. Gareth played cricket with both Ken and Michael; they frequently played on the same side and looked like three peas in a pod when they were at the wicket. Ken as wicket keeper, Michael at first slip, Gareth second slip or gully. It was quite and achievement for them, some of the score sheets make good reading, either bowled or caught or stumped Brawn, then when Michael and Ken were batting the opposition didn't stand much chance. I have seen Michael score 50 off 23 balls in a cup match. He was a joy to see. I remember once when we were touring in Wales, Ken was keeping wicket as usual and Michael was at first slip, as usual when Ken caught a super catch way down leg side. Michael shouted, "Well caught Dad", much to the delight of the spectators and when they were walking off the pitch a spectator was heard to say "Well caught, Dad". Both Ken and Michael were delighted.

Since Cynthia had moved back to Chadderton, she had a bigger house than us we had started to go there for Christmas Day. When Gareth, Andrew and Deborah were younger they liked to watch the film on Christmas Day, usually The Wizard of Oz. Bernard hated it and wouldn't let them watch. Christmas usually finished up with some kind of argument and Ken taking us home in a huff. This year was the same but the children being older just walked out and left the oldies to it, you can't argue if no one argues back. Mother told me Bernard can be a bit miserable at times, he never agrees with anyone and always seems to be contradictory. He has improved with age and only disagrees with politicians these days.

Michael is still playing cricket and now captains the 3rdX1 teaching the youngsters the rudiments of the game. He still scores quite a few runs but takes more wickets these days bowling his 'tweekers' He is trying to break Ken's record. Ken was still playing cricket until he was 56, now Michael is 55 he doesn't have long to go. He is still very fit and the other year ran The Great North Run which is half a marathon just to see if he could do it and he did. When Ken retired the team was so disappointed they wanted him to be non playing captain from the bench, but of course he said "No" and still coached them for a good few more years.

The next page is taken from the3 Chloride Power Paper showing Michael and all his exploits.

CIBL 'DANGER MAN' CLINCHES BATTERY CONTRACT IN IRAQ

FIGHTER ESCORT STANDS BY FOR EXPORT MAN

A fighter plane escort stood by for action when Mike Brawn, 31-years-old CIBL export manager, flew into Iraq on an important battery sales mission.

The flight, in a dangerous area, was the only way to clinch an order for motive power batteries in time . . .

And it was one more adventure for CIBLs 'Danger Man' who in 13 years with Chloride has so far been:

SHELLED by the Peruvian Navy.
HELD in New York for alleged drug smuggling.
FIRED ON in Colombia by guards.
DEPORTED from Venezuela.

On the latest Iraq mission, Mike flew to Amman in Jordan and then found that Baghdad airport was virtually closed because of the war with Iran. No international flights were going in.

The alternative was a 16-hour coach drive from Amman in a temperature of 123 deg.

Then he found there was one flight, the Royal Jordanian Allia which flew into Baghdad at night, and he managed to get on the plane.

He said: "We took off in darkness, and a colleague told me that they flew a fighter escort for the trip to Baghdad. When we arrived all ground lights were out, and security was very tight. The flight took about an hour."

He completed his assignment in Iraq, arranging for the sale of motive power batteries which will power fork lift trucks in food distribution warehouses.

Then there was the problem of getting out of the country . . .

MIKE BRAWN

Said Mike: "If it had not been for the help of our agent in assisting with formalities at the airport I would still have been stuck out there. There were throngs of people at the airport waiting to board the plane and queues at the ticket office — the one ticket office for the whole of the country.

"I managed to get on the plane, arrived back in Amman around 3 am, and immediately boarded the airport bus for the London flight."

Mike has had his share of adventure in his work for Chloride.

Shelled

He was stopped by guards when travelling to a copper mine in the Andes two years ago, and then found that the mountain road was closed. Peruvian frigates circling off the coast then started a bombardment of a nearby target area, first with uncharged shells, and then with live shells, some of which burst close by.

On another occasion, he had flown into Colombia with an arm Officials were finally convinced that he had no drugs and allowed him to go.

In New York, he had flown in on a plane from Colombia, and was again suspected of drug-running. He was interviewed by an FBI man, and allowed to go. But people following him from the plane were arrested.

On another visit to Colombia, he escaped unhurt when shots were fired outside an hotel and a man was killed.

He was deported from Venezuela because he had not been issued with the correct visa — his first trip into the country — and had to fly out of Caracas on the next plane, to the Caribbean, where his visa problem was resolved, and he flew back into Venezuela.

Said Mike: "After a time, you begin to think like a Secret Service agent, to wonder if someone is looking over your shoulder, or following you.

"I have also learned to travel with just a very light travelling case. It saves so much time when authorities don't have to search through baggage before they are satisfied."

.We never knew what Michael was up to, unless he felt like telling us, I'm surprised they got so much out of him at Chloride.

Chapter 8. CALM BEFORE THE STORM

Andrew, Cynthia's son, was just 11 months younger than Gareth; he thought it was great that for one month in the year he was as old as Gareth. He was a good squash player and played for his club, The Maple Squash Club which won the Daily Mail Trophy. He lived for squash and when he wasn't helping his Dad to repair some car or other, he was playing squash. .Both Cynthia and Bernard played squash, they were nearly as keen as Andrew and played at every opportunity but Deborah was still mad about horses, she became a teacher and went all over England helping with the horses jumping and eventing.

Gareth on the other hand was mad about cricket like his Dad and Michael that is when he wasn't out on his motor bike. We didn't much care for the crowd he got in with on the bikes, but they were his friends not ours so we had to make the best of things. He was going out with a young girl called Susan and when it was his 18th birthday he told us they were getting engaged, neither Ken nor I were very pleased but when Gareth got his mind set on something you couldn't shift it. SO we had a joint birthday and engagement party at the Sports Club. A friend of ours made the cake which was like a book with Congratulations on your Engagement on one page and Happy 18th Birthday on the other. She made an excellent job of it, it looked and tasted very good. Once again we did the catering for about 150-200 guests, more hot days in the kitchen.

Too good to last, he met someone during the cricket season and it was all off with Susan. She took to sitting outside the house at all hours of day and night. We got so fed up with it and asked her parents to keep her away. Eventually she got the message. Ho hum! Loves young dream.

Michael just kept on as usual playing cricket and scoring runs. He scored 80 one Saturday and the 83 on the Sunday in an H.C. Smith Competition.

He really was a superb bat and was known on occasion to bowl and over or two. He had briefly been engaged to a girl called Karen but that didn't last long, she knew nothing about cricket, she was a bit of a flibberty-jibbet anyway and wouldn't have suited Michael at all.

In the winter Gareth was knocked off his motor bike he injured his back and bruised all over the place. We didn't find out till later that he had fractured his spine and it caused all sorts of problems. It was shortly after this that he told us he was going to marry Janet. Oh! BOY. She was 14 years older than him and had a 10yr. old son by some Frenchman or other. Both Ken and I were furious and told him he was far too young and didn't know what he was letting himself in for, you know, all the sorts of things parents say under the circumstances but once again when Gareth has his mind set on something no one but no one can shift it. I'm afraid I really lost my temper with him and did my usual when frustrated, threw things. Mother was best she threw teaspoons; she got pretty accurate with them.

They got married in February whilst he was still 18. I sat behind him in the Registrars Office and he was shaking all over, he didn't know what to do with his hands. I have never seen him so nervous. Why did he have to do it? He wore the green velvet jacket we bought him for his 18th birthday and I had flu'. The last thing I wanted was to go to a wedding let alone my son's.

Michael and Ken were still working at Chloride and getting on with life, I had got a job at the local Off Licence which meant shift work again. some Saturday night and some Sunday but it will bring some extra money in. I am fed up of being broke counting the pennies and looking for bargains. and always waiting for the cheque at the end of the month. Why is it that no matter how hard I try to save up I never do. I know "If you stop smoking you will have some extra cash", that is still according to Ken's Father and Mother You could always tell if there was a good film on. It was quiet in the shop during the film but then when it had finished there was a mad rush to stock up before closing time, then we had to cash up and get the books straight before we could go home.

We had decided at last to sell the house and move to a bungalow, the reason being that the last time I was up the ladder cleaning and painting the gutters, I said it was going to be the last time. Either Ken did it or paid for it to be done, as he had never paid for any decorating to be done the simplest thing was for him to agree to a move. We had had a few people round but they thought the same as me, too small. It was the same throughout the year, we had one or two people looking round but that was as far as it got.

Appointments to view meant that I had to clean the house from top to bottom; at least it had its good side.

The rest of the year went relatively smoothly except with Gareth and Janet. She didn't like him coming to see us, especially me, she said we had an un-natural relationship and she could prove it because I pegged my knickers next to his underpants on the washing line. How ridiculous – I peg Ken's underpants next to Gareth's as well so what does that prove??? She has some funny ideas. Daniel her son is rather odd too, he seems reluctant to mix with the others and is inclined to spit, and I hate that. We tried to include them in things we did but neither of them seemed too keen. We even took Daniel to cricket and tried to get him interested, but if you're not you're not.

Christmas we had a fancy dress party at the Sports Club, which was alright and quite well attended, but I feel sometimes that I am flogging a dead horse getting some enthusiasm into the club members, they just seem to want it all done for them. And so to another year.

For some reason I started to keep a diary, boredom I guess but reading through it helps me to remember what sort of year we had. It was one I would rather not repeat and if I copied it word for word it would be a book all on its own. We got a few people looking round the house, but not many. We had a dog called Solomon, a beautiful black Labrador who was a terror when he was small. We had to get puppy sitters if we went out for the night because if we left him on his own he destroyed things, plants especially. We would get home to a house full of soil, plants and plant pots all over the place. He was bored, bored, bored. He grew up into a beautiful, well behaved dog a gun dog, show him a gun and he would follow you anywhere. He obeyed instructions and knew what you wanted before you did. Mother loved him to bits she would talk to him as if she were having a conversation; I think sometimes she expected an answer

Michael had been to Saudi Arabia, he seems to enjoy the travelling around, his pass port is full of interesting stamps, he certainly gets around a lot with work. He rarely said where or when he was going on a trip, the cricket knew before we did. He had to let them know when he wasn't available for matches, and then everyone wanted to know where he had been when he came back.

Keep going up to see Mother every week and take the dog with me, it is getting to be quite a thing. I drove off from the cake shop with the cakes on top of the car. I had put them there whilst I opened the door; someone stopped me and pointed them out, don't know what would have happened if they hadn't. She tell me all sorts of things, mainly about Bernard, he can be such a pain at times, I guess he is going through the mid life crisis, that is if men have one. He said any one over 50 yrs. should be shot; she will never forget that nor will anyone else and we won't let **him** forget either. Mother told me she will buy him a gun for his birthday. Good job we can laugh about it, he has changed his mind these days..

Mother came to stay with us on occasion for a few days rest; she enjoyed being waited on for a change as she usually did all the cooking and cleaning for Cynthia and her gang. She loved to stay and look after Solomon whilst I went to work and even get the lunch or dinner ready for us., as we were only three when she was with us instead of five at Cynthia's. Ken won't smoke his pipe when Mother is with us as it seems to get on her chest, he tries, bless him, but it makes him ratty.

Michael took Ken to the Rugby at Twickenham so they had some arrangements to make. It has done nothing but rain so they will have to take their waterproofs. They set off early morning and arrived back in the evening, I looked for them on Television but there were too many people for me to pick them out and it rained all day.

Gareth is still job hunting, he lost his job through having to keep having time off with his bad back, Janet seems to think he is swinging the lead and leaving her to provide for them, that isn't like Gareth; he loves to work and hates being idle. He is getting more and more depressed, says he can't handle marriage; there must be more to life than shopping and paying bills. Janet is always tired and so possessive and jealous, I never know what to talk to her about, she is very difficult to get to know.

Gareth finally left Janet, He hired a car to take his things up to Michael's, Michael never said a word, and they must have sorted it out at the club on Monday night. He has even taken off his wedding ring so it must be final, he seems much happier in himself. I fed him as he hadn't eaten since yesterday and as usual Michael didn't have any food in the house. I seem to be spending my time feeding him as he hasn't any money and won't have until he gets a job. First of all he needs some new clothes as all he has seems to be what he stands up in and those are torn. Janet treated him like a rubbing rag, she didn't deserve him.

The rest of the year was a nightmare, what with trying to sell the house, working shifts, running Ken and Gareth to and from Cricket matches and the Sports Club, there was all the trouble we had with Janet. Ken finished up calling her The Witch of Endor, can't say I blame him. My B.P. was up, no wonder, I kept feeling dizzy but had to keep going and doing, if I didn't it wouldn't have got done. If Ken or the boys are ill I can look after them but if I am ill, there is no one. Once I had tonsillitis and was in bed, Ken was doing his best as usual and he called up the stairs, "Are these chips done?" I ask you how was I supposed to know. Mother said, "Just get on with it".

Janet would phone up all hours of the day and night wanting to speak to Gareth, He had asked us to say we didn't know where he was and most of the time we didn't. Then she went through a suicide attempt or so she would have us believe. She told Daniel "If you can't wake me up in the morning get your Grandma and Grandpa" I ask you is that the sort of thing to tell a 12 year old boy? Then when we got to hospital she would let Ken go in but not me. I guess she knew I could see through her and would have told her so, I told Gareth it was just moral blackmail and she got to be very good at that.

One day she and her Father turned up on the door step with boxes of Gareth's things and they just dumped them, she still kept asking where Gareth was. Now he had got a job at Manchester Airport through Cynthia, and somehow she found out. Nice friends we have. SO, what does she do but have a restraining order served on him at work. A day or two later she phones Gareth to say she needed to see him. If he had gone I'm sure she would have phoned the police. All this and the phone calls not to mention following us all over the place, talk about being stalked!!! It felt just like that film which was all the rage at the time, Fatal Attraction, O.K. in films but not much fun when it is on your own doorstep. During this my blood pressure was up and no wonder, I hardly got time to myself and Ken got to such a pitch that if he could have got hold of Janet he wouldn't have been responsible for the consequences. My calm and passive Ken, what has she done to you? I seemed to spend most of my time either feeling rotten or working. The Dr. said my B.P. was up again and to take it easy, no wonder I never seem to have a minute to relax and be myself. The whole thing was putting a strain on Ken & me there were times when we couldn't even speak to one another, trying to sell the house isn't helping, we do occasionally have people round but it has been dragging on for 12 months now and I was beginning to think we would never sell

Cynthia and Bernard went on holiday to see Brenda in America, working at the airport she can get there fairly cheaply; unfortunately the concession doesn't apply to us. Mother came to stay and as usual slept most of the time, she only seems to wake up when the film on T.V. is full of blood and guts. We go shopping and do the baking all the everyday things which get you back down to earth. Gave Mother a rest though, her gall bladder was playing up, no wonder, she loved cream cakes. Trying to get her to stick to the no fat diet is nearly impossible.

Reading through my diary for the year it seems to be full of rain, lines of washing, ironing, running Ken and Gareth here there and everywhere and working, not to mention walking Solomon and going to see Mother. Don't I have a fun life? Comparing the weather then and now doesn't seem to be any different; it rained a lot in those days. Janet was still being a pain, she even wrote to Ken's parents telling them all sort of lies. What they have to do with it I don't know. One of these days she will go away, we hoped. Then she phoned up to say she was pregnant,' a miracle' I thought, and she had contracted German measles so she had to have an abortion. When I told her I didn't believe a word she said it quite took her breath away, no wonder she doesn't like me. Is there no end to her calumny? She phones up so often it was getting ridiculous, I was beginning to wonder how she knew Gareth was at our house, then I discovered she was driving up and down the road and every time she saw Gareth's car outside she dashed off and rang him. Getting wise to her nasty tricks. She went down to Ken's parents and slagged off Gareth, what a thing to do to people who have nothing at all to do with anything she never went to see Cynthia or Mother because she knew if she had she would have been told where to go. All this and trying to keep the house nice for buyers, I am getting more and more tired, my B.P. is up a lot with no chance of coming down under the circumstances. She keeps phoning him at work, so when I told Cynthia she was furious, she feels responsible having got Gareth the job in the first place. I would hate to be in Janet's shoes if and when Cynthia had finished with her. The phone keeps ringing all hours day and night and no one replies, I wonder who that is? We decided to change our phone number and go ex-directory to see if that makes any difference.

Went on holiday to Hornsea and had a great time, what a good chance to wind down after all the kafuffle. Just a long week end but well worth it sitting by the lake watching the birds, and eating fish and chips, it was such a nice change and the weather was fabulous for once.

Finally sold the house in September, now we have to wait for the solicitors to do their thing what ever that is, they seem to take ages and ages over things. Still as we have been waiting for this day for the past eighteen months and watched other people in the road sell their houses after a short spell on the market, we give thanks for small mercies. We didn't' get the price we asked, but then who does? Will have to start putting things in boxes now, who knows when the big day will come?

Went round looking at bungalows, I may finally be getting my wish, no stairs. There were one or two but the one we liked was in Little Lever, it wasn't quite what we were looking for as it had solid fuel heating and no gas so that would mean an electric cooker. Apart from that it seemed to fit the bill and be what we wanted and at the price we could afford Mother said "Couldn't you find one in Darcy Lever, it sounds so much nicer?" If only she knew.

Somehow Janet got our ex-directory number, once again from our so called friends at the Sports Club; she must have twisted their arm somehow. I could strangle 'thing' as Gareth calls her. Can't think of a word strong enough I do hope we aren't going through all that palaver again.

Got the date for the removal, December 11th. At last. Are things going to be better from now on? I wonder. Every thing packed, removal men book all we need are the keys to the house and can't get them till the day of the removal.

Chapter 9 FAR FROM PEACEFUL

The day of the removal was 6" deep in snow, when we went to bed it was alright but when we woke up – snow. The dog loved it. The removal men were terrific and got every thing loaded in the van quick sticks. We finally got the keys about 30mts. before the van arrived at the house. When they unloaded if they couldn't find a place for anything they dumped it in the bath. You should have seen the bathroom at the end of the day; we could just about get to the loo.

The bungalow was just what we wanted, it was said to have three bed rooms but we made the front one into the dining room. We can just about seat 8 round the table, any more and we have to have a buffet. The bathroom was big enough to hold a dance in, well nearly depends on how you dance, the people before us had it painted fuchsia with black wall paper and cabbage roses, the tiles were white. That was the first thing to be altered. The only trouble was the solid fuel central heating with a coal fire and back boiler, hard work every morning lighting the fire, so hot in summer. At least there was a thermostat for the water. We had gas installed later and that made it a lot easier.

This was when we got Scooter, our cat, he was part Persian black and white with long hair. Because of the bungalow, we kept our bed room window open for him to come and go as he pleased which worked very well, mostly. Except for THE night, it must have been about 2.0am when we were woken by a kafuffle. It was

Scooter, he had brought a live starling into the bed room. We dived out of bed. Ken went to get a tea towel to catch the bird in and I tried to keep Scooter away from the bird, Solomon joined thinking it was great fun. Can you imagine us dashing round the room in our night attire, Ken flapping a tea towel, me shooing the cat and dog, the starling flying all over the place. By the way starling poo is purple, just thought you would like to know. Eventually Ken caught the bird and let it out of the window followed by Scooter, Have you heard a cat growl? Things took a while to settle down but after a cup of tea we got back to sleep, it must have been 5.0am./ Boy! What a night.

Things got to normal pretty quickly and all was well until 'thing' got our address from???? She started stalking again hanging around the passage and following us to see if she could find out where Gareth was. In the end he left and went I know not where and don't know even to this day.. Some things are better unsaid. What we didn't know we couldn't lie about.

After 3 months when we thought things were going well Ken was out on a job for Chloride when they phoned from work and told me to ask him to go straight back in to work if and when he got home. Which I did, he came back after a short while saying that he had been given notice. Chloride were dividing the works up and Ken had been sorting out who was going where in his department, only to find out that he had done his job so well there was no place for him in either division. On top of that Michael had been asked to go to Argentina and said he thought there was something going on there, it would be better if they waited to see what was going on.

But they told him that as he had refused to go he was to be made redundant as well. If you remember the war in the Falklands started on April 2nd, two days after Michael had been made redundant; I guess he had sixth sense or something like. Could it get any worse?

Well yes it could. As Gareth had had such trouble at the Air Port and as his job was only temporary he was out of work as well. All three of them at the same time.

It was round about now that Mother had gone to see Brenda in California and got Lakered. Do you remember Laker Airlines? Well, Mother had gone to see Brenda via Laker and it was the time when Laker Airlines went bust, so Mother was stuck in America with no means of coming home, SO I had to take her a ticket didn't I? I went for two weeks and spent the first few night in tears, I was so homesick and if I could have got on the next plane home I would. Nonetheless I enjoyed my visit and saw quite a bit of America. Mother and I travelled home O.K. and got through customs at both L.A.and London no trouble, but when it came to boarding the internal flight back to Manchester I was stopped by customs and asked to unpack my bag. Mother was in her wheel chair at the time and sat sliding lower and lower in her chair, trying to pretend she had nothing to do with me. I knew what the customs were looking for but kept the best till last. First of all I unpacked the lemons which I had picked from Stephanie's tree, then strawberries which were in season in America, then a hibachi bar-b-cue which hadn't been seen in England yet, then a hanging basket made of chain along with make up and other essentials which you need for travel

and a metal box which contained recipe cards. Then out came the gun screw driver set which I had bought for Gareth from Annie Oakley's Gun Shop. All those metal things, they must have thought I was up to no good. Poor Mother just didn't know where to look or what to do, eventually they let me repack the bag and we were on our way home. Lesson – be careful what you but when on holiday. We struggled on through the summer till Ken decided to go back to college and duly made enquiries. He firstly wanted to do a degree in history until he found the reading wasn't to his liking, so he decided to do a diploma course in Business and Finance. This meant applying for a student grant; at least it meant some money was coming in, we had by mow cashed in some of our insurance policies just to keep us going and pay the essential bills, money was getting very scarce. Ken went to Bolton College in September, he was amongst 18, 19 20 yr olds and found it very hard to concentrate at first, then steadily he got back in the grove and enjoyed the work. He became the Father Confessor to some of the pupils; they told Ken things they couldn't tell their own Father.
I decided to see what I could do to earn some money and as all the jobs I had applied for didn't seem to want me, for whatever reason known only to them, their loss. I decided to make soft toys and do Craft Fairs every week end, or as often as I could. It was hard work sewing all week and stuffing toys every night just to make enough to fill my stall. Boxes and boxes filled every spare space in the house, good job we had a hatchback car with enough space to take them to the fairs. I made rag dolls, clowns, hand puppets, teddy bears, soft houses and finger puppets. My biggest sellers

were Troggins, little elf like moveable figures which I designed myself. Most of the toys were my own designs or some which I had adapted, you had to have something different or they didn't sell. Then other stall holders would pinch your ideas so you would have to start all over again.

Mother came with me on the odd occasion but mainly I did the fairs on my own as Ken was either busy with cricket or studying or dog sitting, depending on the time of year. Both Michael and Gareth were playing cricket and I hoped we had finally heard the last of 'the Witch of Endor' Gareth was hoping for a divorce but she was asking for support for Daniel. Cheek! he has nothing to do with Gareth anyway

You would think that life was one disaster after another but there was a lighter side which kept us giggling, like when Ken had finished his exams and came home saying "I feel as if by brain has been wiped clean". I patted his bald head and replied "Poor thing" all we could do was laugh. He loves it when I tease him, someone once said we were like a pair of teenagers and I say "Why do the young think they have all the fun?" We giggle over little things. Things settled down for a while, me doing craft fairs and Ken finished school with his diploma but out of work and loving it. If only we didn't have to eat and pay bills life would be sweet. We didn't get any dole money because "THEY" said as Ken had not been paying his national insurance he didn't have any stamps on his card so we weren't entitled to any. Ken was furious and I was spare, we had to manage on Ken's redundancy money until such time as he could get a job.

Michael had had a franchise selling Landspeed which was supposed to be a miracle for growing grass even in the desert, the only trouble was you still needed water, the stuff itself was a good fertiliser but it soon fizzled out. Gareth was working in Manchester with a recruitment agency, but couldn't do anything for Ken. The trouble was now that Ken had his diploma in Business and Finance he was too well qualified for a lot of the jobs he applied for. Michael had met a young lady called Freda who had a 3 year old daughter called Nicola and the set up house together. Freda had her own import and export business and did the markets selling her stuff, as well as a wholesale shop. Michael had got a job and between them they were doing alright. At least one of them is settled.

Then disaster struck again. Not us this time but my sister Cynthia. Mother told me that Andrew had cancer and was having chemo at Christies Hospital. A nicer boy you could never wish to meet, he was fit as a fiddle or so you would think to look at him. He played squash as I said before, he didn't smoke or drink, at least not a lot, and he went on half marathons and kept himself in tip top condition. Then this happened. Why Oh! Why? He had his treatment and was given the all clear or so they said.

He met a young lady and after a whirl wind romance they got married on his birthday in March but had to come back early from their honeymoon as Andrew was in such a lot of pain with his back. The cancer was back with a vengeance and Andrew died in June at the age of 23 years. I feel so sad especially every year on his birthday; he will always be younger than Gareth no matter what happens.

Ken was still looking for work walking round and round Manchester daily calling in all the recruitment agencies. No luck .Eventually, after 5 years without work he got a job checking T.V. Licences which meant walking round the estates and asking to see peoples licence, The weather was terrible, freezing, snowing raining, and every other kind of ing you can think of. He lost a lot of weight, that is the only good thing I can say about it plus he got paid, not a lot, but something.

Ken's Father was taken to hospital, he had been ill for a while and eventually died of cancer, and I don't think they could have done anything for him if they had found out earlier. He had been treated for epilepsy for ages until they found out that he had pernicious anaemia and the treatment they had been giving him had done more harm than good. When he got on the injections for his anaemic he improved somewhat. If only he had known that Freda was pregnant before he died. It was something they, Ken's parents had always wanted; at last we were to have a grandchild.

Both Ken and Michael were still involved with the Cricket Club, Ken was by now President and involved in coaching the youngsters. Both he and I became qualified cricket umpires and umpired many of the matches. Michael was still batting and making hundreds, he took the odd wicket when asked to bowl. Gareth on the other hand who had been a good fast left arm bowler had had to stop playing altogether because of his back which was starting to give him a lot of pain.

During Ken's spell as President every annual dinner was held at the Sports Club and various speakers were asked to attend, the time when Clive Lloyd was asked was particularly good because not only was Ken President but Michael had won the batting cup, a cup which he won on numerous occasions. If you look closely you will see that they, the newspaper,

have spelt our name right Ken always said that when he got a lot of runs they spelt it wrong and when he was out for a duck they spelt it right, but this time they got it right.

We used to have some very good times at the club. We had a little Cairn terrier, before we had Solomon called Daffy her Kennel Club name was Gemma Joyful Girl and she was both Joyful and Daffy. We used to take her with us and she would sit at the back of the court whilst I played tennis. Then after the match she would sit by our side in the bar, the only trouble was the tables were just about her chin height and she would drink up the spilt beer. When she had had enough she would get on the seat next to me and nudge me going "Huh, huh" meaning "I want to go home now." So we did. For a little terrier she was a very well behaved dog.

After Ken's Dad died his mother came to stay with us for a few weeks, the first thing she asked for was a tin of sardines. His Father didn't like them so she had to do without all her married life. It was a treat to see her enjoy sardine sandwiches. When she stayed with us she couldn't get over how hard we worked, she used to think all we did was play, but with Ken working and me making soft toys she changed her mind and went home a much relaxed person. We used to go to see her every week when we could, so with going to see my Mother and his Mother we were kept pretty busy what one thing and another.

In November Verity was born, she looked just like a little doll in the cot wrapped in her shawl. I loved her right from the word 'go' I made her a Moses basket amongst other things, I knitted my fingers sore and the machine rattled very fast. She was worth every minute. I won't say I spoiled her but came very near to it. Our first and only Grandchild, my love, my life, my future,

Chapter 10 A NEW LIFE A NEW BEGINNING

As you would expect Michael was over the moon with his daughter Freda was so happy with another girl and we were so excited, she was beautiful. Verity, a pretty name for a pretty baby. Why do they call her Vez these days? It's horrible and so not like her.

After Freda came home we went to their house and it was, as usual full of people most of whom we didn't know because we didn't mix with Freda's friends very much. We went to see them one day and walked in as usual only to be greeted by someone asking what we were doing there. I lost my temper I'm afraid and told him, we had more right to be there than he had and as Michael's parents we didn't't need his permission to visit our Granddaughter. It was usually chaotic at Freda's sometimes more than others.

I looked after Verity on three afternoons a week so that Freda could go back to work, she is a real workaholic and can't stay away for long. It meant that I went to see Mother on one of the other spare afternoons I had , good job I had the car because it meant taking Solomon with me wherever I went. Life was pretty full in those days.

Eventually Michael and Freda got a live in Nanny Housekeeper, it meant I did have a bit more spare time to myself but when Freda phoned me up to say the Nanny had dropped Verity I was fuming , it took me ages to settle her as every time I went to put her down she tightened up as if she was afraid of being dropped again., eventually I got her settled and back to sleep. If it were me I would have sacked the Nanny there and then, but no, they kept her on , she made a right mess of brining up baby.

Gareth was by then going out with a girl called Julie, a young Irish girl who didn't quite know what day it was. They were living together in a house near the Sports Club and were talking about getting engaged when Gareth had got his divorce. I never thought that would finally happen, Janet was putting up so many obstacles just out of spite. I never knew such a spiteful person. Eventually he did get a divorce but it took nearly 10 years after he left 'thing'. Whenever I went up to see Mother these days she seemed to spend her time pulling people to pieces, from being such a kind and jolly person she was getting to be 'a grumpy old woman' I put it down to her angina which she had had for about 8 yrs. now and the fact that she hardly saw anyone else to talk to or about. Her rheumatism was getting bad which made walking around hard for her so she didn't want to go anywhere because her feet hurt. I can understand that. Poor Deborah and Bernard seemed to get the worst of it, she hardly had a good word for either of them, and what ever they did was wrong. What Mother said these days was not worth writing about. "Bernard has been skiving off work supposed to have a cold, but he spends all his time outside working on that car". "Deborah wants everything done for her, she expects me to do all her washing and if she thinks I will do the ironing as well, she can think again" Oh, Mother do try to look on the bright side, but after all she is 79 and getting on a bit. She phones up with a pile of shopping which she expects me to get and take up with me when we, Solomon and I, go to see her.

Cynthia took her to see Verity and she grudgingly said she, Verity, was a pretty baby, Mother wasn't too keen on babies, but she said she would knit her some bonnets, guess who she expected to get the wool? Even after a few days when I went to see her she still said how pretty Verity was and what a nice name she had. Mother told me she was "As fawce as a Bogart" meaning a very cute baby, I think!

Christmas was coming fast and I was playing dominoes for the team at the Sports Club with Peter Reah, we made a good twosome and seemed to win most games. Ken played occasionally with his arm twisted up his back. He preferred cards or snooker. He was still down in the dumps as he hadn't got a proper job yet, it had been 8 years since he had worked at Chloride and since then had only worked spasmodically. He was working for Manpower Services, which wasn't a real job but they sent him to firms to help sort out the mess they had got themselves in. Manpower only sent them to one place in the hope it would lead to permanent work, but in Ken's case they sent him to a second. We kept our fingers crossed. The firm was Custometal and after Ken had sorted them out they asked if he would like to be taken on permanently. Of course Ken said "Yes". The pay was £68 per week which was twice what he had been getting on the dole; at last he was getting a wage.

Verity was growing nicely and getting to be at the interesting stage. I was still doing craft fares to see if I could make some extra cash and life was becoming normal. Michael had a good job, Freda had her own business and wasn't short of anything, Ken was working and getting back to his old self. He had been a real pain at times when he was out of work, he liked being at home and doing nothing, his favourite occupation, but he didn't' like having no money.

Mother was 80 in February and we had a surprise party for her, we had all clubbed together to get her a really good pearl necklace, something she had always wanted. Keeping things from Mother could be rather difficult as she couldn't keep her nose out of things. If there was a letter she had to see what was in it, if there was a parcel she couldn't wait to open it. In other words she liked to know what was going on, who doesn't. But we managed it and when the day came she was so surprised when everyone arrived complete with presents and birthday cake. She said "I'm, getting an old b----- aren't I"? We had to agree.

I had a letter from Brenda to say she was surprised to hear about the birthday party, no one had told her. Cynthia said she would tell her but promptly forgot and then denies that she had said she would. Anyway Brenda said she had been having some heart trouble, she had to have surgery a triple by-pass and it took her ages to get to be her old self but at least she is still with us.

Ken was still President of the sports club, he kept playing till he was 56, and then his legs gave out on him. That was when we

both took the umpires exam and started coaching the 'smallie boys' as Ken calls them. We both Ken and I coached the young boys for quite a few years, then I started a Ladies Cricket Team, something I had been trying to do for ages. There was quite a lot of opposition from the men at the Cricket Club but we did get it going and had some publicity It took a time to overcome the prejudice against women playing cricket and some of the men were worse than others, we didn't really get much help from them it was hard work.

Some of the teams we played got a lot of support and if you were in Yorkshire they got even more. It was a lot of hard work; we had to struggle like mad to get the wicket cut and marked out. Not many of the men would show the girls how to do it

Experts and beginners (from left): back, Madge, Sarah, Sue, Mena, Nicola; front, Ken Brown, Mervin Williams, Colin Gradwell.

This picture was taken at our very first coaching session in December 1987 just before Christmas. We had one of the regular coaches from the school to show the girls what to do, the reporter from the paper tried her hand at batting and bowling we had quite a good session and it resulted in getting a good few new members for the team. Christmas was the same as always with a little tension but not so much as before, Now that we have Verity things have changed a lot, Michael stays with

Freda and the girls and we didn't see him or them until way after Christmas and thinking about it he hadn't been to see us since last Christmas what with one thing and another. We had done all the running up and down to Prestwich

This was the year when Cynthia and Bernard decided they both had had enough of shifts; they were going to buy a shop, a post office/newsagent's shop of all things. Everybody told them what hard work it would be, but no, they had decided and when they decide dynamite wouldn't change their minds. Eventually they moved out of their lovely bungalow in Bamford to the shop in Worsley. Christmas, what a time to move. It took a lorry for Cynthia to get all her plants, where they put them is anybodies guess as the shop only has a yard. The shifts there were worse than at the

airport as she had to be up every day at 5.0am. for the papers and then be ready to open the post office at 9.am. It was hard work, very tiring and they only got Christmas Day off as the shop was open for papers every other day. It was round about now that Ken and I became Cricket Umpires and as usual the papers got wind of things, not one to shun publicity they came round and took the very unflattering picture. At least it kept the Ladies Cricket team in the news.

Gareth had moved to Birmingham with Julie and had a recruitment agency with his partner. It was quite near the Belfry Golf Club and in a very pretty part of the area. He and Julie had a big falling out and she left. He eventually met a girl called Claire and eloped to Gretna Green, not one to do things by halves. He soon found out that her father was in prison and her brother was no better than he ought to be so she got kicked into touch. Then his partner left him high and dry, running off with all the firms' money. Gareth had no alternative but to go bankrupt. It wasn't a very good time for anyone, so the least said the better. He disappeared to London, can't get much further without falling off the bottom of England.. I miss him though being so far away, I like all my family together in one place.

This was when I was awarded the trophy for starting the ladies cricket team and won £250.00 toward kit. It made all the difference when we started to play in the summer as we had all we needed. Ken and I had fun getting the kit together but getting someone to be responsible for it was another matter.

I still visited Mother, but this time it was because I was working at the shop for Cynthia on Friday mornings, killing two birds with one stone so to speak. It wasn't too bad and a least it meant I was getting a little extra cash; Ken was still working at Custometal the pay wasn't all that much. I had got used to being short of cash and hardly spent any more than I had to, I stayed there till I was 60 then I had had enough. My neck and shoulders had got stuck through doing all the sewing for the Craft fairs and I was going for physiotherapy every week, even now I can't turn my head much from side to side and as for up and down, forget it.

My little Verity was growing up fast and now going to school, Nicola was ready for Grammar School and getting to be a young lady. When Verity was 5 Freda and Michael split up, for what reason I know not, nor did I ask, it was none of our business but Verity wanted to understand why she had two houses to live in. One with her Mum and one with her Dad, trying to explain to a 5 year old about relationships isn't very easy but I managed it somehow and she was content with my explanation. We had her most of the summer holidays and enjoyed every minute, she was a love and very easy to be with. She and Solomon were firm friends and if she had any problem she would put her head on Solomon's shoulder and tell him all about it. He would guard her with his life. We took her to the cricket to see her Dad play, unfortunately she was allergic to some things and I had to carry antihistamine cream round with me, it usually cleared things up fast, but she was worse with cats and rubbed her eyes till they went black. I thought she would grow out of it but she hasn't.

This time I took up woodwork at night school and made all sorts of things for the house culminating in a 'conservatory' as we call it, though it is more like a lean to green house. Verity was about 6 when we were putting it together and I showed her how to use the electric screw driver, she liked to help. We find it very useful now as I grow all my seedlings and cuttings ready for the hanging baskets and tubs not to mention the garden. I missed it when the powers that be decided to close the class down for economic reasons, just when everyone was half way through a project. Mother was slowly getting older and older in her ways; she wasn't getting out much these days and went in a wheel chair when she did as her feet couldn't take her weight. Ken's Mother was the same, she was 6 years older than my Mother but had always been active, playing bowls till well in her eighties between us we spent a lot of time going to see either one or the other, I would clean the house for Ken's Mum and he did the garden. The when we went to see my Mum it was a case of listening to all the woes and troubles. Then eventually they both finished up in hospital, not both at the same time but one after the other. Ken's Mother died in September and my Mother died in November of the same year. We felt as if when we got in the car all we had to do was say "Hospital" and the car would know which way to go. Two funerals in such a short time. Brenda had been over to see mother and was with her for part of the time she was in hospital but had to go home unfortunately just two days before Mother died so she missed the funeral. She felt it badly.

Round about now was when Ken decided to stop smoking; he had smoked a pipe from being in the army and smoked my cigarettes as well. He just said one morning as he was helping make breakfast that as he hadn't had a smoke since 8.0pm the night before he may as well stop altogether. And he did, just like that. If it was hard for him he hid it pretty well and he hasn't had a smoke since that day. I still smoked cigarettes until 2 years later when I had a terrible cough and said I would stop smoking too. Oh! Dear. I became agoraphobic and couldn't go out anywhere. It took me three months before I took up courage to venture out and only then with a tube of polo mints in my hand, clutched tightly.

Gareth had started his own firm in Chingford where his new wife Lisa lived. Lisa had a daughter called Chloe who loved Gareth to bits. His firm did very well. Too well in fact and as it was International it tended to keep him awake at the oddest times. Lisa was a nice girl and easy to get on with, we had some good natters when she came up with Gareth. They stayed with Michael as we have only room for one extra in our bungalow.

Michael had met and bought a house with Julie, an assistant head teacher from Rochdale, she is a wonder girl. Verity and she get on very well together like two sisters in fact. Both the boys seemed settled the only trouble was Gareth's back wasn't getting any better, it stopped him from doing lots of things, but as Mother said he just got on with it.

Ken was by now 70 and had been retired from work before he was 65 as the firm he worked for decided to give his job to their son who had just come out of university. We were now living on a pension which I must say was more than we had before. Then Ken got chicken pox, can you believe it? Chicken pox at his age, I ask you?. It was so painful and debilitating, all down the side of his face. He looked like the man in the iron mask. He was in the isolation ward for a week, both Michael and Julie were surprised to see him in the hospital, he was not a pretty sight, with the mask all down one side of his face, it had turned black when the blisters were drying up. Whenever he wanted anything, the nurses would just open the door and fling it in not wanting to enter if they could help it. Then they sent him home and I had to make sure he was comfortable, there wasn't much treatment and it was just a case of waiting for the pain to subside. He would walk round the bed room slapping his thigh saying every swear word he could think of, very un-Ken-like, then he would have a drink of tea. It seemed to settle him down, and then he would go to sleep in my arms. Good job he had some strong painkillers otherwise he would have been going round the bend, me too. It left him feeling weak all over and his immune system was shot to pieces.

As ever, everyone came for Christmas , we had fun making out the menu as Cynthia is a Celiac, Bernard can't eat dairy products, Julie is a vegetarian, but will eat fish, I can't eat broccoli, considering there were only 10 of us that doesn't leave many 'normal' people. One of the best years was when Gareth came up with a B B gun which could shoot most things without harming them. Unfortunately Michael said "Let me have a go" and promptly aiming it at the Christmas tree shot the finial to pieces. Glass fragments all over the place. You should have seen his face, it was a picture, and he hadn't known he could be so accurate.

Then it was our Golden Wedding Anniversary, my how time flies, fifty years, can you believe it, where had the time gone? We decided to have a garden party.

This is how the garden looked for the Garden Party, pity you can't see the colours, just use your imagination.

Chapter 11 HAPPY TIMES

The Garden party was a huge success. We had caterers in; this was one time when I wasn't going to do it myself. The garden was set out with six tables with golden lace cloths and balloons, we has two pasting tables under the pergola filled with wonderful goodies, and the caterers did us proud. Everyone came, except Verity who was on holiday with her mum, wouldn't you know. When we were setting everything up in the morning it looked like rain and Ken was his usual gloomy self moaning about it. He had become a bit of a pessimist since his chicken pox, but he couldn't help it. The weather did clear up and we had a wonderful day with some of the guests staying till well into the night as it turned out to be a balmy evening as well. Michael gave a lovely speech and the wine  flowed. No unwanted relations this time. It was perfect. No one would let me do anything; Ken was still feeling a little fragile after his chicken pox, but we had a fine time and frequently look at the pictures, pity Brenda and Ken couldn't be with us. We couldn't have asked for anything better. The boys, Julie, Cynthia and Lisa were great helps, they wouldn't let us do a thing and Michael made a lovely speech. Bliss, contentment ruled. Cheers everyone, thank you for a lovely day.

Ken and I had got foot loose and fancy free since the dog and cat had disappeared, poor things. Solomon was 10 yrs old when we had to have him put to sleep, his arthritis was so bad he only had one good leg. Poor boy you could see the pain in his eyes. Pity, he was a great dog. Scooter however was 18 yrs old and had got to be a cantankerous cat only coming in for food. He would stay outside even in the pouring rain. Stupid thing.

So whenever we felt the urge we would go out for the day, Southport becoming our favourite port of call. We could get the train from Bolton and be there well in time for lunch. Another place was the Lake District, it took a little longer but when the weather was good it was worth it. Sometimes we ventured to Chester and had loads of other places on the list.

Ken took up sailing boats and became a member of Bury Marine Modellers, he would sail the boats and I made them for him. He finished up with three radio controlled yachts and a speed boat, they took up most of the room in the spare bedroom. I also made dolls houses and furniture which also took up a lot of space. I still have two of the houses the biggest is a Georgian house with three stories fully furnished and lit from top to bottom.

Another of his passions was golf; he finally got his dream, as the Chloride had presented him with golf clubs when he left. It took him a while but he had lessons and joined the golf club nearby. He enjoyed it and tried to get me interested but it wasn't my thing, as they say. I did try but it was not a good time for me, my feet decided to be stupid and I finished up with orthotics to help me walk. If I hadn't got them I don't know how I would have managed to get around, they certainly helped.

It wouldn't have been so bad if Ken had not had a thing about water; he seemed to fall in where ever he could find it, after his boats or after the golf ball. The trouble with falling in after the golf ball was the water was muddy, and how. He would come home to the back door dripping and say "I've done it again" as if I couldn't see he had, I don't know what either his Mother or mine would have said if they could have seen him. I know I said "That is the sort of thing little boys do, isn't it time you grew up?" We had another fit of giggles.

I was still doing cross stitch, it kept me sane whilst I was stopping smoking, that and painting water colours. The walls are full of my pictures of one type or the other. Ken says "We will need an extension if you do any more". I've stopped for the time being, that is till I have finished writing this epic.

Times were improving, the years were slipping by without any trouble, and the garden was getting better every year. We took a great pride in our garden and people commented on how nice it was. It was peculiar in that the main garden was at the side and we could only see it when we were in it or from the spare bed room window. Nonetheless we had it looking good all through the year. At one time we had 32 hanging baskets and goodness knows how many tubs all around. When we had the gutters changed to plastic we had to cut down on the hanging baskets to 21, it made looking through the windows easier.

Life was sweet, life was fun life was getting better; in spite of us getting older we were enjoying ourselves. Too good to last.

It was round about this time that the pain in Gareth's back got to such a stage that he couldn't stand or sit without painkillers. He decided to have an operation to help things. The only trouble was that if he had waited for the N.H.S. he would be held in a queue of 18 months to two years, he couldn't wait so long, the pain was too bad. He went private at great expense. He had an operation which entailed putting a titanium rod down his spine, could have been very tricky.

The operation was on Tuesday and he sounded in so much pain when I spoke to him on the phone. We went down to see him on the Saturday and after a while chatting, we could see that he was alright, he just got up off the bed and started straightening the bed clothes, we were amazed. He had had a plastic jacket from shoulder to thigh for support and had to wear it for 6 months. The difference it made was amazing, once he had got rid of the armour plating he was back to his old self if not better. Money well spent. When he had been home for 3 weeks Lisa left him, we knew she had bought a flat and we thought she was doing it up to let out for some extra cash, but no, it was to be her new home. Funny but they have been better friends since the divorce than they were before. Chloe still loves Gareth to bits and would rather be with him than her own Dad.

We got along nicely and went on one or two holidays over the next few years. We even went to Italy on the spur of the moment, to a place called Cattollica near Rimini. Beautiful, the weather was so hot we melted on the way down to the beach. Things were perfect. I was still having trouble with my feet but the orthotics made such a difference. Michael and Julie were happy in their house and Gareth had had enough of the rat race. He decided to sell every thing, which meant the house the 2 cars, the motor bike, the boat in Majorca and of course the business.

He turned up at our front door with a back pack and little else. and said he was off to Sri Lanka for how long was anybodies guess. He stayed with us for a couple of weeks then he was off. Our means of communication was by text (I had to learn how to do it) the occasional phone call and the internet. We got along fine.

He was going to come back for Deborah's wedding in August but there was a hitch with the arrangements as Dee, Deborah's fiancé hadn't finished the paper work for his divorce, they should have asked Gareth how to do it. As Gareth had already got the air ticket he said he may as well use it and pay us a visit, though he seemed to spend more of his time away with his friends. He went to Amsterdam and then to Spain.

Ken had mown the lawn and we had had our evening meal. We sat watching television and got ready for bed when Ken said he had a pain. It got worse and I sent for the emergency Doctor, thinking he had got renal colic gain. The Dr. gave him an injection to help him sleep and I had a funny feeling so I sent for Michael. He hadn't been with us long when Ken collapsed. His breathing was odd and he was staring into space not seeing or hearing anything. I told Michael to phone 999 but he just stood there not knowing what to do. In shock I suppose, so I got the ambulance on the phone and they were with us in 15 mts. Good job too for when they got Ken to hospital it was found that he had a ruptured aorta and would have bled to death in another half hour.

The Doctors were marvellous and had him on the operating table in quick sticks. The literally patched him up, it took 6 hours for the operation and he had to have 22 units of blood. Pretty drastic. The he was put in I.C.U. for days. To make matters worse ha had a stroke all down his left side and looked so blown up I felt if you stuck a pin in him he would have fizzed round the room like a burst balloon. It was touch and go for weeks. We had to send for Gareth to come back from Spain and he was a Trojan giving me support and transport all the time. Michael and Julie came every day and so did Verity. Even Freda came and made him some of her Chicken soup.

Ken had been intubated for the first three weeks and then had a tracheotomy which made eating a pain. At first he would only eat soft food, and who can blame him? His favourite was chocolate mouse or tiramisu with iced tea or milk shakes to drink. He lost so much weight and went down to 10 stone; you could count all his ribs, not like my Ken at all.

The worst time was when they phoned up at 6.am to say they were transferring him to Wigan, what a pain that was, they kept him sedated all the time he was there and only gave him 25% chance of recovery. Poor Gareth couldn't take it, Michael was not too happy either, I hoped for the best and didn't loose my belief that Ken would come back to me; it was the only way I could cope. Gareth stayed with me for the first three week, he was a treasure and took care of most things, me included. After the time he was with me he had to get a job to keep his head above water and ended up working in Woking, which is quite a mouthful if you say it quickly. He comes to see us as often as he can and has got the job of I.T. Director which can't be bad. When Gareth went to work Michael picked me up every day to take me to the hospital, I don't know how I would have managed without the boys.

Ken went into hospital on Sept 1st and was there until Nov. 24th. Whilst he was there it was Verity's 18th birthday, she didn't want a big birthday party so we had one for her in the Hospital dining room. All the nurses attended. The best bit was when Ken walked in the dining room to Verity. She didn't know he had started to walk and burst into tears "Oh, my Granddad, my Granddad" It was very moving and you couldn't have had a better birthday wherever you went. Julie worked hard to get the food right and the nurses finished up with the birthday cake.

Before he was allowed home we had to have a visit from the occupational therapist to see if things were suitable for him to come home to. Ken would have flattened them if he had had the strength. He said they treated me as if either I was a servant or I wasn't there. One of them was South African and I may as well not have existed, she didn't seem to see me at all and I wasn't included in any conversation or any part of the things Ken would have to do when he came home. BUT we kept our mouths closed as we didn't want to rock the boat. They came on Tuesday and Ken came home on Thursday. Boy, were we relieved.

We were both so happy when he came home even though it was hard work for me, it was far better than having to go to hospital every day, not knowing how he would be. Now I could see for myself and make sure he was alright. The fun, if you can call it that was when he fell and I just couldn't get him up. He fell in the lounge, he fell in the bed room, one time he fell in the bathroom and I had to get Michael to come to help me pick him up at 6 o'clock in the morning, he had cut his head slightly and there was blood everywhere, you know how badly heads bleed.. At least now if he falls he can get on his hands and knees, crawl to a chair and get himself up, it is a relief for me and my shoulders.

The physio came to see him after he had been home 3 weeks and I had already started on his workout, some ballet and some yoga exercises, they seemed to work O.K. The physio was surprised at how well Ken had progressed. He came for 6 weeks and then signed Ken off and left the rest to me. Now some 8 months later he can walk without the Zimmer and on occasion without a walking stick. He does try to be too ambitious and do things he shouldn't and I tell him off for doing it, but at least he is here for me to tell him off. I still get very tired as it is hard work looking after him 24 hours a day, but who cares I love him.

Deborah's wedding was in the January after Ken came home, we all went to a very happy occasion. Michael was best man and Gareth was the supporter as Dee had no family in England, him being from Barbados. Deborah looked beautiful and Ken managed to walk up the aisle to his seat. He had been using a wheel chair prior to that. We had a taxi home and Ken was pooped by the time we arrived home, the spring had wound down.

We are aiming now to go to Morecambe for our 56 wedding anniversary in July as we 'eloped' there last year without telling anyone we were going, we are hoping to have lunch in The Honey Tree Chinese Restaurant and a walk down the Promenade to the Eric Morecambe statue,

We made it, even though we were on mobility scooters.

CONCLUSION

This started out as what my Mother told me but as time goes by her reminiscences became mine. I can remember her telling me to keep my independence because once you have lost that you have lost your way. If you have to rely on other people too much you will never get things done.. She felt this when she sold her house to go to America, for when she came home she had nothing of her own it hit her hard though she never told anyone of at least I don't think she did.

So do it yourself and if you can't do it yourself get the best person for the job to do it for you. I have done many things in my life but the best thing I did was to marry Ken and have my two fine boys. They were a bit of a pain at times but worth it in the end. Then there is Verity, my treasure, Ken's sweetie, what more need I say. Every one is pictured here except Verity; she is far too busy these days. We do see her on high days and holidays though, and

Deborah's husband, Dee who had to go back to Barbados for a while.

Since writing this my big sister Brenda died in June 2007 and Ken has had a further stroke and fractured his hip (on our holidays of all times) He now walks with a three wheeled walker and life goes on as usual.
Next year is our 60th Anniversary and I tell him I will swap him for a newer model. As if?